Praise

"Enlightening, revealing and essential reading for every workplace, boardroom and leadership team to reflect on and make a change to have more women represented."
— Angela Tomazos, Vice President, Australian Federation of Business and Professional Women

"Representation matters, especially in the workplace, as it reflects the world we live in. This is an essential read for any organization looking to empower their people to sustainably embed a culture of diversity and inclusivity."
— Roshni Hegerman, JAPAC Enterprise Lead, Oracle, and Founder, Pinch of Masala

"A game-changing work on crafting a gender-diverse workplace from the voices of those in charge."
— Irene Natividad, President, Global Summit of Women, and Chair, Corporate Women Directors International

"An indispensable read on diversity, equity and inclusion (DEI) that expertly blends research-based insights with compelling personal journeys and corporate interviews, making it the only guide you'll ever need."
— Tess Mateo, Sustainability ESG Impact Investor, US W20 Delegate to G20, and UN Advisor

"The must-have manual by exceptional leaders for helping navigate from why to how in achieving gender equality."
— Nicola Corzine, CEO, Nasdaq Entrepreneurial Center

From Bias to Equality

How Business Leaders Can Drive Innovation, Success and Profitability by Embracing True Gender Balance

Sandra D'Souza

Foreword written by Ann Sherry AO

R^ethink

Barry and Allegra, the loves of my life

Contents

Foreword

I've always been an advocate for gender equity in workplaces and I know how difficult it has been to make the progress we have to date; I think change is too slow. We need to understand what is getting in the way of the logic that shows that more equitable workplaces and gender-balanced teams create better business outcomes.

When Sandra asked me to write the Foreword for her book, I was intrigued by her work interviewing other CEOs who have championed for women represented on boards and in C-suite roles.

Sandra is part of this "special" network advocating for gender equality for the past twenty years. She started at the grassroots level as an executive committee member of the Sydney Chapter of BPW (Business and Professional Women), then in 2006 was elected as New South Wales President. She later was appointed to the executive board of the International Federation of BPW in 2012. She has spoken at events such as the Global Summit of Women in Tokyo in 2017, where I am on the International Hosting Committee. Sandra's passion also extends to entrepreneurship around women founders.

As we move toward a more inclusive and equal world, it is imperative that we address and confront biases, especially in the workplace. This book sheds light on the issue of gender bias and provides valuable insights and practical steps toward achieving gender equality in business. Sandra has done a wonderful job of presenting the complexities of this issue in a comprehensive and thought-provoking manner. This book serves as a call to action for business leaders and individuals alike to become conscious of their biases and take meaningful steps to confront them to create a more equitable work environment.

I highly recommend this book to anyone looking to promote gender equality in their leadership teams... and I think that should be all leaders.

Ann Sherry AO

Introduction

It was October 2022 and I had just attended a business event hosted by one of the most progressive CEOs in the world. He had wowed the audience with his diversity and inclusion policies, but then made a puzzling statement when we were talking afterward – "It will take some time before we see women in C-suite roles, let alone CEO or CFO roles, because they need time to have children."

I couldn't believe it. It was late 2022 and here he was saying that women needed more time than men to reach these positions. This seemed archaic in such a modern leader. Still, I could tell from his expression that this wasn't an intentional slight against any gender; rather he saw this as an unavoidable truth based on his experience.

While his statement seemed out-of-place among all the progressive ideas he shared throughout his speech, I couldn't help but notice the reaction when I relayed his words to others which was split between agreement and shock. Those who agreed seemed resigned to the fact that progress takes time; however, those who reacted with disbelief thought it outrageous that such views were still being held by business leaders in late 2022. In a way, it saddens me that, despite our cultural progress over recent years, outdated views still persist, even among influential leaders such as the speaker.

Obviously, his statement is not the case: there are countless examples of successful women who are capable and skilled in their professional and executive careers and who also have a family. So how could one rule them all out for simply needing to have time to have children? That seemed unfair at best, and downright discriminatory at worst.

This story isn't meant as a judgment on anyone's perspective, but rather a reminder that we as women still face many invisible barriers in securing C-suite leadership roles whether it is about motherhood, the color of our skin, or unconscious bias. Despite being half of the population, women are still visibly underrepresented in senior leadership roles.

The reason behind the book

I have been advocating for gender equality, either as a corporate business executive in an informal capacity or as a volunteer for an International NGO that has a special consultative status with United Nations, for over twenty years. As a result, I am across research as well as policies and initiatives implemented at local and international levels. I've also attended numerous conferences discussing the lack of progress and the barriers for women over those years.

The Covid pandemic has proven that businesses can survive with their entire workforce working from home and that workers can be just as productive, if not more so, when working remotely. So, in late 2021, my team at Ellect (www.ellect.biz) and I embarked on our research journey to see how much we have progressed with gender equality in senior leadership roles, such as on boards of directors and in C-Suites. We decided to look at all the Australian Stock Exchange (ASX) companies and read through their publicly available information. We awarded one point to the company for each accomplishment listed below:

1. Have at least one woman as CEO or CFO

2. Have one woman board chair

3. Have at least 25% women on the board of directors

4. Have at least 25% women on the senior leadership team

We set the gender criteria at 25% of representation for women representation in the board of directors and C-suite leadership teams. However, the ideal range for gender balance is 40% to 60%.

For each company that has scored at least three points, we consider them to have achieved gender equality in business leadership. The theory behind this is that, historically, there have been few women in C-suite roles such as CEOs, CFOs, CIOs, and board chairs of listed companies. However, with the significant increase of work in diversity, equity, and inclusion, we thought we would finally see greater representation of women at the most senior levels.

At the time of our research and analysis in early 2022, we rated over 2,100 companies on ASX and continued our work to rate over 8,800 companies on NASDAQ. You can find our results on Ellect's website.[1]

After rating all of them, less than 5% of companies had achieved three points or more! In ASX, only ninety-eight companies have achieved three or four points, and in the NASDAQ we found 203 companies that have achieved the same. I was dumbfounded by these results. It's hard to believe that in the year 2022 there are still shockingly few women occupying leadership roles in business. Despite making up over half of the population, women continue to be underrepresented and lack access to powerful positions within the corporate environment. This imbalance is not only disheartening but discouraging for aspiring female leaders.

I am a fan of using emojis and this is where I would type in a lot of screaming faces.

It's time to start taking concrete steps toward real progress and greater representation of female talent across all levels of business. We must keep pushing for a more equal-opportunity workplace where everyone has the same chance of success regardless of their gender identity.

How could this still be?

Two things happened when I was faced with these results. First, we launched Ellect Stars as a straightforward accreditation process. The criteria (being the four accomplishments listed above) are straightforward with no ambiguity. You either have achieved them or you have not as a business. There are no subjective views, and we celebrate companies that have clearly embraced gender balance in senior leadership.

The second thing I did was to contact the CEOs of the ninety-eight ASX companies that had scored three or more stars to find out how they achieved it and what makes them the minority among their peers. Fortunately, many agreed to be interviewed. I ended up interviewing thirty-four, including eleven whose interviews form the second part of this book.

The key observation across all of the interviews is that they have one thing in common. Regardless of whether the CEO is a founder or recruited into the role, has a large or small market cap, is in a male-dominated industry or not, or has offices in Australia or across the globe: the companies are all committed to diversity at every level of management. More importantly, they do not see it as a compliance requirement or pressure imposed on them to achieve diversity. They are pioneers in pursuing diversity because they believe that in order for their organization to succeed, they need diverse thinking in their boards and leadership teams.

It may seem like I have given away the answer at the introduction of the book, but there are also strategies that they have shared with me which I have summarized in the first part of this book. This section is designed for you to read in one sitting with the detailed interviews forming the second part of the book.

If you have been struggling as a business leader to bring gender balance to the most senior level of management, I promise you that by reading the strategies and the interviews, you will have the confidence to push for gender balance in your C-suite team and on your board of directors.

PART ONE
STRATEGIES FOR ACHIEVING GENDER EQUALITY

Do You Truly Believe In Gender Equity?

Gender equity is increasingly becoming a mainstream topic of discussion. However, many people are talking about it, but few actually believe in it. There are still too many companies that lack gender diversity and gender parity in their leadership teams.

As a leader in your organization, do you really believe in gender equity?

I ask this question because I have experienced many conversations with people that start off with the best of intentions. They tell me they are supportive of diversity and have an interest in helping women to access opportunities, but then it becomes glaringly obvious that their views are colored by their unconscious bias.

People like this may not have malicious intent, nor are they necessarily trying to limit opportunities for women – they simply don't recognize the biases formed within them due to long-standing societal norms and cultural influences. Admitting such instances of unintended prejudice can be difficult; however, this admission is a step we must all take if we are to create diverse workplaces.

It's likely you have heard the term "unconscious bias" thrown around – in this book, business discussions and other publications. But what actually is it? Unconscious biases are assumptions we unknowingly make based off our past life experiences or cultural stereotypes which form mental shortcuts to help us quickly process information. These can be so embedded within us that they shape both limiting beliefs and behaviors – impacting how companies hire, interact with colleagues, and even decisions made by leadership teams. Left unchecked, these deep-rooted biases can negatively affect company culture and prevent progress in bringing gender equality and diversity into the workforce, and more importantly, into leadership teams.

Perhaps a relatable example for you to quickly understand the negative impact of unconscious bias is the gender pay gap. To this day, the gender pay gap occurs in all countries and societies and across most professions. The gender pay gap might seem like an individual problem – of a man simply earning more than a woman because of merit, experience, or some other legitimate factor – until you look at the data.

The gender pay gap occurs worldwide and in nearly all industries and professions, regardless of objective factors that should influence income, according to the World Economic Forum (WEF). Globally, women earn on average just 69% of what men are paid for the same work, and just 40% on average in countries with the least gender parity.[2]

If we are just looking at data, have you reviewed your company to see if there is a gender pay gap? Even though you personally believe that men and women are being paid equally at your organization, it is best to confirm this with actual data considering that gender pay gaps do exist in almost every organization in the world.

Keren Paterson, CEO of Trigg Mining, shared her personal experience with the gender pay gap:

"My first experience was following our first summer vacation period at university. On returning to campus, I learned that many of my male colleagues had been paid twice what I received. We were doing the same work, with the same level of knowledge and experience.

"I also experienced this in my first graduate role. There, I was paid a base salary from head office and it was up to the sites to 'make up' the salary gap between the graduate rate and the operator rate for the work that I was doing. I knew that other male graduates that had worked at that mine before me had received the top-up payment. I stated my case and asked to be topped up to the lowest level trainee operator in the mine for the duration of my time working as an operator, no matter what work I was performing. I was told that I was 'getting "my time" toward my FCMCC [First Class Mine Manager's Certificate of Competency] and I should just be grateful.'

"On a third occasion, I was employed to project manage a feasibility study on a new underground mine. Not long into the role, I was asked to take on the management of the mining operations in addition to overseeing the feasibility study. This new role required my FCMCC and had statutory accountability. I benchmarked the role (it was paid 50% more than the feasibility role), prepared my case for a pay rise and negotiated as hard as I have ever negotiated. I wasn't asking to be compensated for doing both roles – I was simply looking for the industry standard for the statutory role, where I was now leading a team of 150 people, managing a multi-million-dollar budget and was personally accountable for their safety

(I could have gone to jail if something terrible had gone wrong). The response – I was getting experience and I should just be grateful…

"I would also like to mention that there were notable exceptions in my career where my gender had no bearing whatsoever on what I was paid. In these situations, they saw my skills, knowledge, experience, drive, and grit for what they are, and what I could do in achieving the company's objectives. They paid me accordingly and fairly. These are the men I am grateful to have worked for."

In 2019, Medtronic, a global medical device company, joined a handful of companies sharing information about pay equity.[3] They actively addressed the issue and reportedly achieved 99% global pay equity by job title and 100% in gender pay equity across employees in the US.

While it's easy to think that unconscious bias is someone else's problem, the truth is that we are all susceptible to its effects. As we've seen, these biases can have a significant impact on our work and personal lives.

The good news is that there are things we can do, like the work of Medtronic tackling the gender pay gap, to mitigate the biased influence.

The question remains: do you truly believe in gender equity?

If your answer is yes, I urge you to start by looking at the data on the gender pay gap. Even if you think there is no issue with how men and women are paid at your company, it's important to get an accurate picture by looking at the numbers.

And if your answer is no, well, that's a whole other conversation.

Unintentional Bias

Professional women have shared with me a discouraging pattern of discrimination in their workplace conversations with CEOs and other business leaders. While this isn't an attempt to redefine unconscious bias, these accounts show how pervasive the issue can be.

I often have conversations with professional men who argue that men and women cannot be equal because of physical differences. One example was a former military person who claimed that his women colleagues could not carry 50kg backpacks like the men and therefore gender equality is impossible. Actually, I received many explanations that equality can't be achieved even in a professional setting due to the physical limitations of women.

However, I came across an example that would challenge this broad-brush claim when I watched an episode of the *Big Brother* TV reality show by chance earlier in the year. I am not a follower of this show, so I am giving you a sketchy overview. It is a show about twenty contestants who live in a house with cameras filming them twenty-four hours a day for seven days over a few months. They have many physical contests to compete in and the winner receives a prize that gives them additional "power" or advantage over other contestants. In the only episode I happened to watch, there was a physical contest where the participants needed to endure hours in a standing pose holding onto ropes and balancing on a swing. After a few hours, after almost a dozen others could not maintain the physical requirements, it came down to two contestants – a physically fit twenty-five-year-old man versus a fifty-two-year-old woman. The woman contestant won, beating all the contestants who were younger men and women in a physical endurance challenge. I thought it represented a great example, that you cannot always assume gender inequality on the basis of physical differences.

The other example I shared at the beginning of the book is often presented as a basis for why women cannot achieve the same level of leadership roles as men: because women need to take time off to bear children. It is a limiting belief imposed on women, as you will see if you read the interview in part two of this book, with Judith Mitchell, who has successfully led an executive career from the 1980s while being a single mum due to the supportive work environment that allowed her to fulfill her potential and accelerate her career. She is an inspiring leader and a great role model.

Is it easy to stereotype women and form limiting beliefs about them? Yes, and if you are guilty of this, you could be hurting your company.

If you need a little more proof of the negative impact of unintentional bias, here are some statistics:

Statistics related to diversity and gender bias in the workplace by builtin.com:[4]

- 42% of women experience gender discrimination at work.[5]

- In 2022, 59% of women said they had experienced harassment or microaggressions at work in the past year.[6]

- 93% of women say they fear that reporting non-inclusive behaviors at work will have a negative effect on their careers.[7]

- Globally, almost 50% of people believe men are better political leaders, while more than 40% see men as better business executives.[8]

- In the fiscal year 2021, 18,762 charges were filed with the US Equal Employment Opportunity

Commission for sex-based discrimination. Those complaints led to more than USD150 million in payouts.[9]

- Both men and women are twice as likely to hire a male candidate.[10]

- Women are seventy-nine times more likely to be hired when there are at least two female candidates in the finalist pool.[11]

- Half of the men believe women are well-represented in their company, while 90% of senior leaders are men.[12]

- Men are 30% more likely to obtain managerial roles.[13]

- Women and men ask for pay rises at the same rate.[14]

- Women receive pay rises 5% less often.[15]

- Companies with executive teams in the top quartile for gender diversity are 25% more likely to see above-average profitability.[16]

- 5% of CEOs globally are women.[17]

- Women represent just over 28% of boardroom seats.[18]

- 19.2% of C-suite roles are filled by women.[19]

- 4% of C-suite roles are held by women of color.[20]

- 15% of CEOs at Fortune 500 companies are women.[21]

- As of 2021, women of color made up 1.2% of CEOs at Fortune 500 companies.[22]

With a world increasingly focused on equality, it's so important to recognize where unconscious gender bias in the workplace exists. Looking at startling statistics such as those above will help you understand the impact of limiting beliefs imposed on women and how they could affect your company – like not being able to achieve leadership roles due to taking time off for parenting duties. By actively looking into these biases, and with dedicated attention and effort, businesses can take steps toward reducing them.

Why You Need
More Women Leaders
In Your Business

A s a woman, I'm passionate about shaking up the status quo and advocating for equal representation on boards and leadership teams. Doing so isn't just morally right, it's also smart business. Research has consistently proven that companies with diverse executive teams outperform those run exclusively by men. For example, S&P Global research revealed that companies with women CEOs and CFOs have a 20% boost to their stock price momentum within twenty-four months of an appointment – significantly higher than average performance compared to markets at large.[23] Furthermore, when businesses embrace such diversity, they are more likely to be profitable, socially responsible, provide higher-quality customer experiences and enjoy numerous other advantages – making it clear why so many organizations should strive for greater representation among senior leadership roles. This financial advantage should no longer be overlooked or ignored – instead, it should be embraced as an integral part of achieving success at any modern company.

Further evidence came from research across India, UK, and US-listed firms, which showed an undeniable material difference associated with including women on company boards, clearly indicating its importance for business growth prospects.[24]

Companies that achieve greater gender diversity are also more likely to make better decisions, be more innovative be better able to manage risk, and are better able to attract and retain top talent. This is because today's employees want to work for an organization that values diversity and is committed to promoting equality. By achieving gender balance in your organization, you're sending a strong message that you're an employer of choice – which will give you a competitive advantage to attracting and retaining top talent.

This is one of the reasons why we established Ellect Stars badges (www.ellect.biz/). We've established these badges of excellence to recognize an organization's commitment to true gender parity. These awarded companies showcase their dedication by exemplifying a strong representation of women in senior leadership roles, providing an opportunity for ambitious talented female professionals seeking out "women-friendly" workplaces and rewarding career progressions.

"Holman Webb is always committed to achieving gender equality. We made sure our progress was measured on a regular basis so that we could track how we were going compared to other organizations in our industry.

"In 2020, we established an Employer of Choice committee. The committee's purpose was to achieve various goals, including improving diversity and inclusion. We asked staff undertaking various roles in the organization to participate and put themselves forward if they wanted to be committee members. We had equal male and female representation, and some short-term goals were to actively recruit and develop the existing female staff and remove unconscious biases.

"During the recruitment and promotion process, the long-term goals were more ambitious. We wanted to achieve, by 2024, a 5% increase in the number of senior roles held by females. We also wanted to achieve greater gender equality at the partner level and improve diversity and inclusion.

"What was great about this process was that all the goals came from the employees, which we put into the strategic plan and presented to the management. It was very structured and had a clear purpose regarding what we wanted to achieve, timelines, how we were going to measure, as well as a plan on how we were going to report on our progress."
— Magdalena Kosior-Molloy,
    Chief Operation Officer and Chief
    Financial Officer, Holman Webb Lawyers

Women professionals may be frustrated with the lack of diversity in top leadership roles within companies. One reason is that it can create a feeling that the company has a "glass ceiling," an invisible barrier preventing women and other underrepresented groups from advancing to the highest levels of leadership within a company. Women and other underrepresented groups may feel that their contributions are not being recognized or that they are not being given the same opportunities for advancement as their white male counterparts. This sends a message that certain groups are not valued or respected within the organization, leading to resentment, frustration, feelings of exclusion and marginalization, and ultimately to a lack of motivation to stay with the company for the long term.

Additionally, when a company lacks diversity in its leadership, it can also create a culture in which employees from underrepresented groups do not feel comfortable or included. They may feel that their ideas and perspectives are not being heard or valued, which can lead to a lack of engagement and motivation. This can lead to a lack of innovation, creativity and problem-solving, which can negatively impact the company's overall success.

Furthermore, when individuals from underrepresented groups see mostly white males in top leadership roles, they may feel like they do not belong and that they are not welcomed in the organization, which can lead to their disengagement and even loss of talented professionals.

Let's assume that you have been trying to recruit more women into senior leadership roles but have not been successful. How do others find the woman leaders you are looking for? You may have found the following reasons (or excuses) for not succeeding:

- "Women are not applying for the senior roles we advertised."

- "Women are not interested in board or senior roles."

- "There aren't that many women with the right credentials and depth of experience to sit on the board – the issues covered are extremely complex."

- "Most women don't want the hassle or pressure of sitting on a board."

- "All the 'good' women have already been snapped up."

- "We have one woman already on the board, so we are done – it is someone else's turn."

- "There aren't any vacancies at the moment – if there were, I would think about appointing a woman."

- "We need to build the pipeline from the bottom – there just aren't enough senior women in this sector."

- "I can't just appoint a woman because I want to."

If these "reasons" resonate with you, then you are reading the right book to help you address them.

Finding qualified women candidates for top leadership roles is a challenge that many organizations face. But the good news is, it doesn't have to be so difficult. By understanding the areas where companies hit roadblocks, it's possible to craft an effective strategy that yields great results.

The range of business leaders I interviewed was varied, though the majority were from listed public companies. The industries were also varied – financial services, mining, professional services, software, biotechnology, oil, and gas. The CEOs I interviewed included both founding CEOs and those recruited into their roles. Regardless of their origins, they implemented their approaches to achieve gender balance. The size of the companies varied too, from a small mining start-up to an international IT services company spanning four continents.

I have compiled the best practices of some of today's pioneering business leaders who have found success in recruiting women onto their boards of directors and senior executive teams. Through interviews with these same executives, I have uncovered strategies and advice to provide insights and guidance to overcome any obstacles that prevent organizations from recruiting women into leadership positions. By following their example, you can also take steps toward creating more equal representation on your board or executive team.

Five Ways For CEOs To Drive Change For Gender Equality

As any business leader knows, a company is only as good as its employees. That's why it's essential to carefully consider the composition of your team, ensuring that you have a diverse group of people with the skills and knowledge necessary to help your business succeed. This is especially important when it comes to leadership positions. A diverse team of leaders can bring different perspectives and experiences to the table, helping to make better decisions and foster a more creative and innovative environment. This view is supported by many of the business leaders I interviewed, including the ones I didn't include in this book.

Here's an extract that supports this view from my interview with Benn Lim:

"One of the many steps to building exponential organizations [ExO] is the team composition, where diversity is an important part of the package and particularly so for community-driven companies. Furthermore, to deliver diverse backgrounds, independent thought, and complementary skills, roles such as the visionary/dreamer, user experience design, programming/engineer, and the finance/business roles are critical in ExO teams.

"This makes a lot of sense, because tackling problems requires creativity and innovation which can only come when we have different perspectives from a diverse group of unique individuals from different backgrounds."
— Benn Lim, Chief Operating and Impact Officer, Arowana

Progressing toward gender equality is not going to happen overnight – it will take time, effort, and commitment. But it can be done.

Here are a few things you can do to get started:

1. **Assess current status:** Conduct a comprehensive audit of the company's current policies and practices related to gender equality. This should include data on the gender breakdown of employees at all levels, as well as any existing

programs or initiatives aimed at promoting gender equality. Extend your audit to survey your employees to understand if they are experiencing limitations due to lack of diversity.

2. **Develop a strategy:** Based on the findings of the audit, develop a comprehensive strategy to achieve gender equality within the company over the next three years. This should include specific goals and objectives, as well as a plan for how to achieve them.

3. **Implement policies and practices:** Put in place policies and practices that promote gender equality, such as flexible work arrangements, parental leave, mentoring, and training programs.

4. **Increase representation of women:** Develop targeted recruitment and development programs aimed at increasing the representation of women in leadership roles, as well as in positions that are traditionally male dominated.

5. **Monitor and evaluate progress:** Regularly monitor and evaluate the company's progress toward achieving gender equality, and make adjustments as needed.

6. **Hold leaders accountable:** Hold leaders and managers accountable for promoting gender equality and creating a culture in which women are respected, valued, and heard.

7. **Communicate and educate:** Communicate the company's commitment to gender equality to all employees, and educate them on the importance of diversity and inclusion in the workplace.

8. **Encourage employee engagement and feedback:** Encourage employees to engage and to give feedback, and take steps to address any concerns or barriers that may be preventing women from achieving equality within the company.

9. **Create a support system:** Provide support and resources for women within the company, such as mentorship and networking opportunities, and provide training on unconscious bias and how to address it.

10. **Incentivize progress:** Reward progress toward achieving gender equality within the company, and recognize the efforts of individuals and teams including the CEO who are working to promote diversity and inclusion.

It's important to remember that gender equality is a continuous process, not a one-time event, and will require an ongoing effort to maintain and improve over time.

In order for true progress to be made, it is important for CEOs to take an active role in driving change within their organizations. The leaders I interviewed are aware of this need and are committed to creating gender parity within their companies. They were essentially consciously biased. While they discussed with me many ways to achieve this goal, there are five methods that stood out the most:

1. Assessing your values and beliefs.

2. Securing support from the board chair.

3. Incorporating targets and values into the strategic plan.

4. Empowering your leadership team.

5. Understanding the importance of diverse and inclusive interview panels.

One – Assess your values and beliefs in gender equity

A workplace that is considered "women-friendly" is an indication of a healthy, progressive company culture. Women face unique challenges in the workplace and it is important for businesses to recognize the need for gender equality and inclusion.

As a business leader, do you care about gender equity? After all, wouldn't you like to see more women in senior leadership roles? Do you believe in providing additional opportunities and support to underrepresented groups? If you answered yes to these questions, then gender-equity initiatives are something you should implement in the workplace.

By taking part in these initiatives, you can help create a more inclusive workplace environment where everyone has an equal opportunity to succeed. With your support, the next generation of female leaders will be inspired to reach even higher levels of success. Ask yourself, what's holding you back from championing gender equity in the workplace?

One of the interviewees shared his reasons why it's important to champion gender equity:

"… the real driver of our success is our diversity in terms of males and females and culture. You need different perspectives. That's what makes a company great. Still, there's undoubtedly a different female-male mentality as well. You'd be very foolish to undervalue the different perspectives: that's like saying I'll listen to my father, but I won't listen to my mother. That's just dumb. I have been and am still influenced by many strong females in my life, starting with a very strong mother and grandmothers. My mother was an only child and always wanted lots of kids. The eldest child in my family is my sister, another force, so my brother and I were influenced by strong women. In my family, all the vocal parties were women, not the men. The men were strong, silent, and supportive."
— Daniel Lai, CEO, archTIS

As a business leader, you need to ask yourself – can I always be committed to gender equity in the workplace? Do I strongly believe that everyone should have an equal opportunity to succeed, regardless of gender? Can I therefore be supportive of initiatives designed to promote gender equity in the workplace?

Essentially, all of these questions lead to the real question: what is the true workplace culture you are leading? Here's another insight:

"Culture is the essence of building a healthy and strong company. It is the personality of the organization, and it really starts from the top and inculcating the right values top down and filtered down through the organization, with our senior management, middle management and leaders of our operations living and breathing the same mindset. We as management have to practice what we preach and, leading by example, to continue to inculcate the correct culture, behavior, and values in our organization.

"My mother has built over the years strong company values of integrity, trust and loyalty and treats every colleague as though we are one big Ghim Li family. We recognize the value in treating each and every individual with respect, no matter their position. As a result,

we have a very strong loyal employee base
and continue to attract talent who value such
a company culture."
— Felicia Gan, CEO Ghim Li Group

Recent research by McKinsey has provided more evidence that, by advocating for policies that provide additional opportunities and support for women in senior leadership positions, creating a more diverse and inclusive workplace by ensuring that your employees are hired from a wide range of backgrounds can help create a more productive and successful workplace.[25] By promoting gender equity in the workplace, you can attract and retain the best talent, build a more innovative and collaborative workforce and, ultimately, improve your bottom line.

If you don't, inequality can come with a high price tag. Without the right policies in place to combat inappropriate conduct and discrimination, toxic cultures often persist within workplace environments. Even some of those seemingly minor HR practices, like offering benefits or recruiting potential employees, may play into these issues if they don't treat people equally – particularly when they deal with gender-based discrepancies or milestone events such as childbirth. Just recruiting women leaders is therefore not enough, especially if they cannot flourish in your workplace culture or leave.

You are now likely well aware of the importance of gender equality inclusion and the need to create an equitable workplace culture. As a leader, it is your responsibility to lead by example and take the necessary steps to ensure that gender equality is embraced in your organization. To help empower you as a business leader, I have outlined five actionable steps that will help you kickstart gender equality inclusion in your workplace culture:

1. **Assess if you have unconscious bias:** The first step toward establishing a successful gender-equality inclusion program is to evaluate yourself for unconscious bias. Unconscious biases can be difficult to recognize and may even be unintentionally shaped by past experiences or cultural influences. To assess if you have any, try creating a list of assumptions about women or their roles in certain positions within your company that could present barriers to equal opportunity or advancement. This exercise can help you identify any potential blind spots or areas where unconscious bias may be present so that you can proactively challenge those preconceived notions when making decisions about hiring, promotion, and other personnel matters. You can also undertake a well-known Project Implicit Association Test (IAT) (https://implicit.harvard.edu/implicit/takeatest.html), an online tool to gain greater awareness

about one's own biases, preferences, and beliefs. Alternatively, you can try our Gender Unconscious Bias Personality Test (https://bias-test.com) which is designed to help you gain a deeper understanding of your personal biases and attitudes toward gender.

2. **Listen to the lived experiences of underrepresented employee groups:** The second step is to talk with underrepresented groups of employees in your organization and truly listen to their stories and experiences as they relate to gender equality inclusion efforts at work. By engaging with these individuals on an individual basis, you can gain valuable insight into how they feel about existing policies or what changes would make them feel more supported or included in your organization's culture. Doing this will also help them feel heard and appreciated for their unique perspectives, as well as build trust between leadership and these individuals, which can only serve to strengthen any existing gender-equality inclusion programs already in place.

3. **Demonstrate your commitment to gender equality:** In order for your team members to take your commitment seriously, it's important that you show them through actions rather than just words. Create policies that support working mothers, offer flexible working hours for all genders, and ensure equal pay across different

positions within your company – all these steps will demonstrate your dedication to promoting gender equality in the workplace. Additionally, make sure that any new hires reflect diversity – this will allow everyone in the company to feel respected and valued regardless of their identity or background.

4. **Create a workplace that supports women:** You have the power to action much-needed progress in gender equality. Take steps toward creating a better work environment for women in leadership roles, such as implementing maternity-leave policies that are not career limiting, or considering qualified women with children as candidates for promotions. Encourage men in leadership roles to take paternity leave to set an example that family responsibilities are not limited to women only.

5. **Terminate inexcusable behavior:** It doesn't matter who it's coming from – if someone is behaving inappropriately, either verbally or physically, then they need to face consequences immediately so that everyone else understands what language/actions are unacceptable in the workplace. Make sure that all employees understand what behavior is expected from them when interacting with colleagues from different backgrounds and genders; this way there will be no room for confusion or misunderstanding when it needs to be enforced in future situations.

These five steps will set you off on the path toward becoming an inclusive leader who contributes positively toward creating a culture based on gender-equality inclusion within your organization. However, true success depends not only on making sure all these steps are taken, but also sticking with them over time – encouraging constant dialogue around this topic (at all levels), continuously evaluating progress made against set goals and objectives and remaining open-minded when introducing changes.

Two – Secure support from board chair to achieve gender balance

The quest for gender balance in the boardroom and senior leadership team can be fraught with challenges. Without the support of the board chair, it can be difficult to achieve gender balance. The board chair needs to be committed to the vision of gender equity and gender equality. They also need to be willing to hold the rest of the board accountable for gender balance. Without this support, it can be more challenging, although not impossible, to achieve gender balance.

> "A respectful relationship between a chair and CEO is essential to running a successful company. The CEO is a representative of the board, and if there are opposing values or views on the direction of how the company needs to run, it can be disastrous. No one

wins, or worse, the company ceases to exist. I am fortunate to be working with a Chair who believes in supporting the CEO; I've worked with many who did not. It can be exhausting running a company with multiple stakeholders, especially in a highly regulated industry like ours. The addition of subversive turmoil and dealing with competing agendas is just unnecessary. The job is difficult enough."
— Annick Donat, CEO, Clime Investment Management.

A good working relationship between the chair and CEO is therefore essential for any successful business organization. The chair is the bridge between the board of directors and management, and the CEO is responsible for carrying out the board's decisions and directives. In order to effectively collaborate on achieving gender-equality goals, it is important that the chair and CEO have a clear understanding of each other's roles and responsibilities.

"... I was never worried about the board's reaction. Partly because I have strong alignment in objectives with a very supportive board, but more importantly, I came into the role knowing that the board was proactively seeking change and transformation. Given my background, I think the board and I knew that it was a period of transformation for Link Group and that's what I was brought on

to do. To that end, I have never been afraid to challenge the status quo, set a new agenda and vision, and mobilize the right team to get us there."
— Vivek Bhatia, CEO Link Group

The key to gaining the support of a board chair is communication and collaboration. While the CEO owns the strategy, it is important for the board chair to be informed about it and given an opportunity to give their opinion on it. This can lead to the rest of the board members supporting the CEO's gender-equality initiatives.

If you have a board of directors that may not be open to gender-equality initiatives, these eight steps may help to gain their support:

1. Clearly outline the benefits of gender-equality initiatives for your company, such as improved employee retention and satisfaction, increased diversity and innovation, and a positive impact on the company's reputation.

2. Provide data and research to support your arguments, such as studies showing the positive correlation between gender diversity and financial performance.

3. Highlight any relevant industry trends or best practices and explain how implementing

these initiatives will help the company stay competitive.

4. Emphasize the importance of diversity and inclusion as a core company value and explain how gender-equality initiatives align with this value.

5. Show how the initiatives will be implemented and the return on investment.

6. Have a clear and well-structured plan of action, including specific goals and metrics for measuring success.

7. Build relationships with the board of directors and board chair to understand their interests and concerns, and address them in your proposal.

8. Finally, be prepared to answer any questions or address any concerns that the board may have and be willing to make adjustments to your proposal as needed.

While gaining the approval of the board may not always be easy, demonstrating transparency and openness throughout the process can go a long way toward establishing credibility, which can ultimately lead to successful outcomes down the line. By proactively communicating with board members throughout your planning journey, you can give yourself a better chance at winning over their confidence and garnering meaningful buy-in from them when it matters most.

Three – Incorporate targets and values into your organization's strategic plan

There's no denying that gender inequality is still a problem in the workplace. Despite the many advances that have been made, women are still being paid less than men for doing the same job, they are still under-represented in leadership positions, and they are still bearing the majority of the burden when it comes to balancing work and family responsibilities. In order to change it, organizations need to commit to achieving gender balance at all levels, including the board of directors and senior leadership team.

One way to do this is to set a goal for gender equity in your organization. This means that you are committed to ensuring that there is an equal representation of women and men at all levels of the organization. To reach this goal, you need to incorporate specific actions into your strategic plan, including recruiting more women into leadership positions, providing training and development opportunities for female employees, and promoting flexible work arrangements that allow both women and men to balance work and family responsibilities.

"… Businesses are made up of people like you and me, and we all have things that matter to us in addition to our jobs. When we were going through the process of articulating OZ Minerals' purpose, we asked ourselves: what's that special 'something' that makes us who we are, why we like being at OZ Minerals and what helps us connect to our personal why? The outcome of that is our purpose statement that reflects a higher order, the 'why we get out of bed each day' that helps define OZ Minerals and everyone who is part of our business.

"Because OZ Minerals' purpose was jointly created by the board, executives, company-wide leadership, and people from across our business, it became something that resonated with our people and helped to bring meaning and real direction to our work.

"We have also consciously taken steps to sharpen our focus on improving gender equality and inclusivity in our workforce and leadership over the last year and a half through a series of system changes."
— Andrew Cole, CEO OZ Minerals

Four – Empower your leadership team to implement gender-equity initiatives

Creating gender-equity initiatives is not a one-person job. It takes buy-in from senior leadership, and just having their support is not enough – they need to lead these initiatives. Empowering your leadership team to implement gender-equity initiatives is an important step in demonstrating a commitment to change. By allowing your team to take the lead on these initiatives and make sure that the necessary steps are taken, it increases the chance of success that gender-equity goals are met and that everyone feels included in the process.

To truly create an environment of equality and fairness within your organization, it's essential for leaders at every level – from upper management to individual employees – to understand how each decision affects gender diversity. This means having honest conversations about why certain decisions are being made and ensuring everyone is on board with any changes.

Leaders can create a supportive environment for their teams by setting clear expectations for behavior around issues like workplace attire or language used when discussing gender topics. Additionally, organizations may want to provide resources for employees, such as offering training workshops focused on understanding unconscious biases or providing informational materials that outline company policies related to gender diversity and inclusion.

"I recall in my younger CBA [Commonwealth Bank Australia] days, one of my bosses was preparing a workshop for the team and asked me, 'What do you want to know?' I said to him, 'I don't know what I don't know.'

"Hence, for me, having a framework that enables me to formalize my understanding as well as to identify where more learning is required is essential.

"The B Corp certification process in the first instance is a corporate awakening moment to see how much we do or do not do, and then we can start to fill in the gaps. Like all awakening moments, when we discover a better way of being, that is when our journey begins.

"All companies who are committed to becoming a certified B Corp need to go through the B Impact Assessment (BIA). The BIA focuses on five key areas of impact, which are Governance, Workers, Community, Environment, and Customers, and brings to light questions within that need to be considered, some known, some not, and some that should have been known.

"The BIA reviews our diversity, equity, and inclusion within the Community area of impact by assessing if the company is led by individuals from underrepresented groups; what practices the company has in place around diversity, equity, and inclusion; what diversity metrics we track; the number of women; the number of managers that are

women or from an underrepresented social group; and the number of board directors that are women."
— Benn Lim, Chief Operating and Impact Officer, Arowana.

Ensuring that your organization's leadership team is committed to implementing these types of initiatives requires more than just having an awareness of their importance. It needs a deep understanding of how ingrained gender biases can be in organizational cultures and how they impact the experiences of both men and women in the workplace. To ensure that your leadership team can implement these initiatives effectively, it is important that they receive appropriate training on topics such as diversity, inclusion, pay equity, and unconscious bias. This will allow them to develop an understanding not only of what needs to be done, but also why it needs to be done in order to make meaningful progress toward achieving gender equity in the workplace.

In addition to training on topics related to gender equity, it is important that leaders are provided with clear goals when it comes to implementing such initiatives so they know what is expected from them. They need to be given access to resources that provide guidance on how best to implement such measures so they can make informed decisions about what works best for their organization's unique context.

Leadership teams should be recognized when they successfully implement gender-equity initiatives as this will help create a positive feedback loop which encourages others within the organization who may not have initially been convinced by its importance or efficacy. This reinforcement should take place both internally (through awards or other incentives) and externally (by sharing successes with media outlets or other external bodies).

It is vital that, throughout all stages of implementation, leaders ensure that there is an ongoing dialogue between managers and employees about how their work life could potentially be improved through such initiatives if implemented correctly. By giving individuals a platform through which their voices are heard, leaders have an opportunity not only to demonstrate their commitment but also empower employees by allowing them a sense of ownership over any changes being made, as well as creating a space where open dialogue about equality issues can take place without fear of retribution or exclusion from colleagues or management teams who may not share similar views on these issues.

"The implementation plan (and its continued evolution) has been very much an internal endeavor. Our People and Culture team generate and manage the plan, with many of the initiatives coming from collaboration across

the company – through focus groups, empathy interviews, and qualitative feedback from Peakon, our monthly engagement survey. The executive team reviews progress against the plan each quarter and the board once a year."
— Mike Bennetts, CEO, Z Energy

Allyship

Have you heard of "allyship" as opposed to "mentoring"? If not, here's a quick explanation – allyship and mentoring programs are both aimed at supporting individuals in their professional development, but they have some key differences.

Allyship programs are focused on creating a culture of inclusion and equity within an organization. They are designed to educate employees on issues related to diversity, equity, and inclusion, and to provide them with the tools and resources they need to become effective allies. These programs are often targeted at marginalized groups, such as women and people of color, to help them advance in their careers.

Mentoring programs, on the other hand, are focused on providing individuals with guidance and support from more experienced professionals. Mentors can provide mentees with advice, feedback, and guidance on a wide range of professional development topics, such as career advancement, networking, and skill development. Mentoring relationships are typically one-on-one and can be formal or informal. They are usually targeted at individuals who are early in their careers and looking to develop their skills and advance their careers.

Both can work together to help individuals achieve their professional goals and create a more inclusive and equitable workplace, but allyship programs can better help implement gender-equality initiatives since they are designed to create a more inclusive and equitable culture within an organization.

I believe that an allyship program is a proactive initiative aimed at fostering a culture of inclusion and equity, particularly with regards to gender equality. If you are considering implementing such a program, here are some steps that your organization can take:

1. **Establish clear goals and objectives:** Define specific and measurable goals for the allyship program, such as increasing the representation of women in leadership positions or reducing the gender pay gap.

2. **Identify key stakeholders:** Identify key stakeholders, such as employees, leaders, and external partners, who will be involved in the allyship program and work to engage them in the initiative.

3. **Develop a comprehensive training program:** Create a training program that focuses on

educating employees on issues related to gender equality, such as unconscious bias, privilege, and intersectionality. The program should also provide employees with the tools and resources to become effective allies.

4. **Create a system for tracking progress:** Establish a system for tracking progress toward the goals and objectives set for the allyship program. This will help identify areas where the program is succeeding and areas that need improvement.

5. **Establish accountability:** Hold leaders and employees accountable for the success of the allyship program. This can be achieved through performance evaluations and other forms of feedback.

6. **Create a safe space for dialogue and feedback:** Create a safe space for employees to have open and honest conversations about issues related to gender equality, and to provide feedback on the allyship program.

7. **Make it an ongoing effort:** The allyship program should not be a one-time event but an ongoing effort, where everyone continuously works on it and makes adjustments as needed.

This last point is important to note; implementing an allyship program is an ongoing effort and requires continuous support from leadership and active participation from all employees. Regularly evaluating the progress and effectiveness of the program is crucial to make sure it is meeting the goals it set out to achieve.

"People often quote, 'treat people the way you want to be treated.' I don't think that is correct; I think it is more effective to 'treat people the way they want to be treated.' You are managing a group of different people who have different communication styles, different learning styles, and different values. Yes, you can align the values, but to get the best out of each individual you need to match their communication and learning needs and adapt your style.

"The first piece of advice I give to leaders is, when they are making a request of their people, remember to say *why*. Without the why, this is an order not a request; without a why, people don't necessarily see or understand the context; and without the why, how do they link the request to the mission as the links are not always clear? I remember once sitting on a plane as it landed in LAX, and like most planes it was running late. There had been a medical emergency on the plane, and they needed to get the EMTs on board but the aisle was full of passengers trying to jockey to get out. The flight attendant asked twice for people to remain seated but the aisle was still packed – and to be fair the rest of the passengers could not see the EMTs at the front of the plane. I said to the attendant – tell them why you need them to sit down – and immediately after the announcement the aisle cleared.

"We have a belief in Next Science – if we all know the why around the actions, we will all make aligned decisions."
    — Judith Mitchell, CEO, Next Science

Ultimately, no matter what changes are put in place within an organization, it's important not only for leaders but all employees within the company to recognize their role in creating an environment where gender equity is encouraged and respected at all levels throughout the organization. By engaging everyone involved in these initiatives you can ensure success now, as well as long-term sustainability, so that gender equity continues long into the future.

Five – Understand the importance of diverse and inclusive interview panels

One area that is especially relevant for creating gender equality in the workplace is the interview process. Diverse and inclusive interview panels can help to reduce bias and increase the likelihood of finding the best candidate for the job. A diverse panel can bring different perspectives and experiences to the table, which can lead to a more thorough evaluation of candidates. Inclusion ensures that all members of the panel feel comfortable sharing their opinions and that all candidates are treated fairly. This can lead to a more representative workforce and a more positive and productive work environment.

By including team members with lived experiences on interview panels, organizations can get a broader range of perspectives, which can help reduce the risk of bias and ensure that the best candidates are being selected for the role.

"I believe that it has to start right at the very beginning of the recruitment process, and needs to be embedded via a diverse and inclusive culture. For Lepidico, we are building this business from humble beginnings as a start-up. Therefore, part of the brief to any recruitment agent is that we *need* diversity across the organization. For example, in Namibia, where we are currently building an operating team, we want to establish both gender and ethnic diversity among the workforce, while also being in harmony with the community. ... there are tribal considerations in Namibia where there's a significant number of different tribes, which we need to be mindful of.

"There are not a lot of women in the primary industry workforce in Namibia, so it is a challenge for us for recruitment right now. We have developed a recruitment plan to build out our organizational structure over a two-year time frame, and in doing so will identify the roles where we're best able to achieve a diverse workforce. In time, training and succession planning will also be important features to become more diverse. As stated several times now, this drive really needs to come from the top.

"For the roles that I'm responsible for recruiting, the executive management roles, I've been mindful of establishing diversity. If recruiting externally, the brief to the agent is to push for an equal number of female and male candidates, if possible. It does not mean we exclude men but we do emphasize the search for women candidates. For our interview process, we ensure that we also have an equal number of men and women in the final interview and, if possible, throughout the process. Having women in the roles of Chief Financial Officer and General Manager of Sustainability provides a good balance of skills on any interview panel.

"Another example of our proactive recruitment approach is when we needed to recruit for a Country Manager. The interviews were conducted in Namibia and one of the candidates was a standout. It was very clear when I saw her CV that she was overqualified for the role, but she was, on paper, a very good candidate for Sustainability Executive, a role we were also looking to fill. Interestingly, I had a preconceived thought that the Sustainability Executive position would probably be based in Toronto, Canada, where we have one of our corporate offices. However, having this function in Namibia is a much better fit for the business since Namibia really represents the epicenter of our sustainability imperatives. It's where we have our greater sustainability exposures. Having a Namibian woman operating locally at group executive level is just fantastic. We interviewed the candidate, who subsequently came on board and she is an absolute champion. She is brilliant for the role and brings great professional experience.

"Having a woman as one of the most experienced and senior people in the country is going to give us the best shot at having as diverse an organization as possible."
— Joe Walsh, CEO, Lepidico

Additionally, blind résumés can be used to further reduce the risk of bias. By removing information such as gender, race, and ethnicity from the equation, decision-makers are able to focus solely on qualifications and experience.

Another way to make the interview process more diverse and inclusive is by using structured interviews. Structured interviews are based on predetermined questions that are asked in a consistent manner to all candidates. This helps to level the playing field so that all candidates have an equal opportunity to demonstrate their qualifications for the role. Additionally, structured interviews can help to reduce unconscious bias by providing a framework for evaluating candidates that is not based on personal preferences or assumptions.

> "In planning for the recruitment process, I was encouraged by one of the directors not to let the gender balance fall and to search for a woman. I'm grateful he did, as I had been conditioned to think that my gender was something that I needed to balance out with a man in the CFO role. Yes – bias can occur in all of us!
>
> "So, my shortlist was 100% women in this case and, as a company, we are very happy with the outcome.
>
> "For other roles, wherever possible, I've ensured that we have had a balanced shortlist and a gender-balanced selection team to address any unconscious bias we may have."
> — Keren Paterson, Trigg Minerals

Overall, there are several steps that can be taken to implement a diverse and inclusive interview process for recruitment:

1. **Identify and address bias:** Recognize and address any unconscious biases that may exist among interviewers. This can be done through training or by using tools such as structured interviews or blind résumé review.

2. **Create a diverse interview panel:** Ensure that the panel of interviewers is diverse in terms of race, gender, age, sexual orientation, and other factors. This can be done by actively recruiting and selecting a diverse group of interviewers.

3. **Use inclusive language:** Use language and communication that is inclusive and respectful of all candidates. Avoid using gendered or discriminatory language.

4. **Be transparent about the selection process:** Communicate the selection criteria and the process to all candidates. This can help to reduce bias and increase the transparency of the process.

5. **Encourage active listening:** Encourage all members of the panel to actively listen to the candidates and to ask open-ended questions that allow them to share their experiences and qualifications.

6. **Diversify your recruitment sources:** Look for recruiting sources and job postings that reach a diverse group of candidates.

7. **Track and measure progress:** Keep track of the diversity and inclusion of your candidate pools and hires, and use this information to identify areas where improvement is needed and to monitor progress over time.

Implementing these steps can help to create a more diverse and inclusive recruitment process, which can lead to a more representative and productive workforce.

Putting The Strategies Into Practice

In Part One of this book, I share five strategies that can help your organization achieve gender balance. They are:

1. **Assess your values and beliefs in gender equity:** A key step to achieving gender equality is to assess the values and beliefs held by you and within your organization. To do this, the organization should conduct a survey or consultation with employees and management to gain insight into their attitudes and opinions on gender issues. This will provide data that can inform decisions and policies, as well as identify any areas where improvements need to be made. Additionally, it is important for organizations to educate staff on all aspects of gender equality,

so they can better understand its importance and how they can contribute to it.

2. **Secure support from the board chair to achieve gender balance:** Organizations must ensure that their board chairs and their CEOs are committed to achieving gender balance. The board chair should make sure that it is a priority for the board, setting targets for diversity among board members and ensuring the success of initiatives aimed at increasing the representation of women in leadership roles. Additionally, they should promote a culture of respect for all genders within the organization.

3. **Incorporate targets and values into your organization's strategic plan:** To ensure progress toward achieving gender equality, organizations must include targets in their strategic plan which reflect their commitment to gender equity. This could include increasing the percentage of female leaders or decision-makers in the organization, or creating new internal policies for equal pay or parental leave which benefit both men and women equally. Additionally, organizations should make sure that these values are clear throughout the organization by communicating them across teams through workshops or training sessions.

4. **Empower your leadership team to implement gender-equity initiatives:** It is essential that organizations have strong leadership teams

who are willing to take action when it comes to implementing measures to achieve greater gender balance. This includes having senior leaders who model behavior that promotes respect for all genders and taking steps such as actively seeking out female candidates when recruiting new hires, or putting forward targeted initiatives which aim to increase female representation in certain roles within the business.

5. **Understand the importance of diverse and inclusive interview panels:** Having a diverse interview panel is essential if organizations are serious about their commitment to achieving gender balance within their workforce. Diverse panels allow different perspectives on candidates' skillsets, experiences and potential contributions to be considered when making hiring decisions. This includes a range of factors including cultural fit that may not otherwise have been considered due to stereotypes or unconscious biases surrounding candidates' backgrounds or characteristics (eg, race/gender). Furthermore, research has shown that companies with more diversity also tend to perform better financially than those without – likely due to increased creativity stemming from more varied backgrounds among their workforce.

It's also important to remember that achieving gender equity is a critical goal, but it will not happen overnight. Success requires navigating various organizational barriers such as lack of buy-in from senior executives, existing power structures, or challenges associated with changing the existing corporate culture around topics like sexism/harassment, part-time work, working from home, and paternity leave... to name just a few.

Part Two of this book explores the stories and perspectives of some of the inspiring business leaders who have made it their mission to drive gender equality in their organizations. We hear how they identified the need to address the gender balance in their work environment, created plans to implement change, and tracked progress toward achieving gender equity. Overall, achieving gender balance requires dedication, commitment, and hard work – but it is possible for businesses that are willing to put in the effort. The journey may be ongoing, but having inspiring leaders committed to the vision and paving the way provides a clear pathway that demonstrates that equality can become a reality if we strive together toward this goal.

Lastly, be self-aware. Notice people around you. Note the diversity – is it minimal or is there none? Or is the level of diversity in your organization something you can already be proud of? If lacking in diversity, then be consciously biased – that is, be biased to diversity. Be a champion of change.

PART TWO
THE INTERVIEWS

Annick Donat, CEO, Clime Investment Management Limited (ASX:CIW)

With over thirty years' experience in financial services, Annick is an active advocate for helping Australians access high-quality wealth advice and financial education. Her expertise spans governance, strategy, distribution, business and practice development, financial advice, and product management. Annick Donat was appointed CEO of Clime Investment Management Limited on 1 May 2021.

Prior to becoming the CEO of Clime, Annick was the CEO of Madison Financial Group, now a wholly owned subsidiary. With her active and influential voice in the financial services industry, Annick sits on various industry advisory boards and contributes her expertise to several not-for-profit organizations. Annick is passionate about life and learning. She is an avid reader, loves cooking for family and friends, is a mother of two life-embracing teenagers, and finds her most reflective moments in the snowfields or on a yoga mat.

About Clime Investment Management Ltd

For over twenty-five years Clime has been helping advisers, individuals, and trustees, manage their wealth with investments selected by our experienced team. With over $1bn in funds, we are who Australians trust with their money.

Clime was created to help Australians understand, manage and expand their wealth. Since our inception in 1996 by Founder and Chair John Abernethy, we have grown consistently, underpinned by a culture of integrity, transparency, conviction, and progress. Listed on the ASX in 2001, our team of investment professionals has been helping more and more Australians invest confidently. We are an established company with a future focus. We believe in investing in Australia's sustainable future, to support small business owners, innovators, and founders. We ultimately believe in building a better Australia.

Interview with Annick Donat

You were appointed as CEO in May 2021 and yet you achieved diversity in your board of directors and senior leadership team within six months. Could you share the journey of your achievement?

It wasn't on my "bucket list" to be an ASX CEO; however, it was a goal to be a CEO of a boutique financial advice licensee. I set the goal for age fifty and achieved it. Mind you, the first week into the role I had deep reservations and wondered if I'd made the right decision. It was a small business, quite unstructured and with minimal resources. I had spent the last twenty-plus years in Corporate where we had resources, people, and access to high-quality infrastructure. However, I reminded myself why I wanted to do this type of role. It brought me back to the coal face and out of the "ivory tower." The role gave me the opportunity to be directly connected to our clients. I remember thinking to myself, the part I had always loved about being in the financial advice industry was the connection to financial advisers. I thoroughly enjoyed (and still do) working with small business owners who are passionate about what they do and the clients they serve.

So, the first thing I did was get in front of the advisers in our community to learn about their businesses, what they valued from us, and what we needed to improve. This was the fastest and most insightful way to understand our community and their needs, and to set a strategic direction for the company. A former manager once said to me when I first started in a previous role, "Annick, you can spend all your time in the office reading and learning about our products and what we do. But the best way to learn is to get out there and speak to clients." It's a tougher way to learn because you're exposed, may not have all the answers, and are unsure how to solve their issues, but it's an honest way to learn. It's understanding that listening is a skill, and when done correctly, connects with a client more deeply than telling them how much you know. It's also where I started to learn that often understanding the question is far more important than knowing the answer.

All these lessons still serve me today and helped when I found myself faced with a challenge that (at the time) felt insurmountable and beyond my realm of capability and, worse, control. It was January 2020; the world was just beginning to deal with Covid-19 and my previous company was put up for sale after the parent had gone into administration. Among many other things going on, my team and I were thrown into a washing machine of change and uncertainty. Overnight, we'd gone from having the support of a parent to being on our own, with no leadership support (our board deserted us) and we were dealing with administrators, receivers, business brokers, regulators, and the media. There's plenty of public information on how this story ended, so I'll give you the short version. We were acquired by Clime Investment Management Ltd, where I am now CEO.

How I ended up in the role is yet another story, which when played back seems incredible. There are parts of this story best left for conversation because I was taught that "if you can't say anything nice, don't say anything at all." However, I will share the parts of this story that had an impact on how I came to be a CEO of a K company.

The role became available in approximately December 2020. While it fleetingly crossed my mind to apply for it, I quickly dismissed it because of the amount of change and turmoil my team and I had faced in the previous four years and, quite honestly, I was emotionally and physically spent. The thought of taking on a role which required more of my time, in a public arena with heightened scrutiny, did not appeal at all. It seems the Universe had other plans for me.

I'd been listening to the board discuss the type of CEO they wanted, and it was mainly focused on culture and leadership style. It was important for our company to have a leader who was committed to our values and who could bring out the best in our people. There was, of course, the standard skill and experience requirements for this type of role, but the focus was on cultural fit. This appealed for many reasons: Clime's values and ethos of integrity, transparency, and conviction, which had been led by our Founder and (now) Chair John Abernethy, really resonated with me and my team. John is a person who truly believes in helping others understand their financial situation and he has always openly shared his knowledge with others so they can make informed decisions. He is a genuine person who believes that everyone is responsible for making a business better; we are all empowered to be the best versions of ourselves and do the right thing by the client.

The reality of the interview process was somewhat different from John's core values, however, the story ended well for me. Jaime Johns, a leader I work alongside, asked me if I was going to apply for the Clime CEO role. I said no and gave her the reasons I described earlier. She understood how I felt but went on to say, "I think you should apply. If you don't, they'll put someone in the role who you'll have to teach about financial advice and how it works within an investment company, which will frustrate you, and you'll end up leaving. This won't be good for anyone." Still not convinced, I went home and relayed the conversation to Simon (my husband) and he suggested I throw my hat in the ring. In his view, it was an opportunity to learn, go through an important process, and demonstrate I was committed to the company and passionate about contributing. Simon has always been the person

I turn to when I need help making a difficult decision. He's smart, pragmatic, and loves me. I know when he offers advice, it's in my best interest. I decided to have a break over Christmas, give the opportunity the consideration it deserved, and decide upon my return in the New Year.

In January 2021, I submitted a formal application along with credentials, copies of media articles, and videos which I believed provided the best evidence of my ability to be considered for the CEO role. I didn't hear from anyone for a month. There was no formal acknowledgment (just a few words in an email), there was no conversation from any director except for John… there was silence. Behind the scenes, résumés and first rounds of conversations had commenced. To set the scene, I was working from the same office as the directors who were conducting the interview process. In fact, I was in an office next door to one. Yet at no time did he acknowledge my application. You're probably thinking, "Why didn't she follow up?" It's a good question. I assumed that, because I was an existing employee, I would be approached last because "they" knew I was interested and once the field was narrowed sufficiently, I would be approached for an interview. As the saying goes, never assume.

One morning, John called and asked if I'd applied for the role. A little surprised by the question (John was not involved in the initial interview process), I said I had some weeks ago and hadn't heard from anyone.

That was a sliding door moment. John raised this with the director responsible for the process, made it clear it was unacceptable that I hadn't been acknowledged, and within the day I received a response – an apology – but still had to wait a few weeks for my first "interview." It was obvious in my first interview that none of what I'd submitted had been reviewed or read. The questions asked were basic, many of which were unnecessary. However, I went through the process and answered everything asked of me. On a positive note, many of the responses resonated and there were a few light-bulb moments which caused the interviewer to think differently about my application.

Without boring you with all the details, the process to get the role was a test of mental resilience. I was put through more interviews than the other candidates, was asked to submit more papers, and subjected to some very poor conduct throughout the process. All of which I've put behind me, and as Jaime used to remind me when I had lapses of anger, I got the job. I couldn't have achieved this without the support of John Abernethy. He gave me sound advice, including to toughen up if I wanted to be an ASX CEO, and he ensured the recruitment process was conducted fairly.

After I was appointed, it was easy to see the best way for our company to progress and become ready for the future was to review the board and bring in the talent and expertise who had a growth mindset and were prepared to challenge the status quo. This was a big decision for Clime, and one which was supported by our major shareholders. When our company first joined Clime, I had the privilege of meeting some of our major shareholders, and it was evident they believed in Clime, wanted the company to grow, and were looking for change in leadership thinking and direction. I was appointed in May 2021, and by June a board review had commenced led by John Abernethy (now Chair) and a private consultant. Ronni Chalmers, Director and shareholder, was also instrumental in finding the incredible women we have on our board. Ronni is well connected, and he reached out to many of his contacts to get recommendations for board members (male and female). We ended up with about sixteen candidates, and a rigorous selection progress commenced. John and I had discussed the ideal composition of the board, and both agreed we needed diversity across gender, experience, and age. We ended up with the board we have today. Our board is comprised of five members, two female. Industries span politics, academia, law, technology, artificial intelligence, crypto, blockchain, economics, marketing, media, and global and local investment markets. Importantly, all our directors are self-made. They know what it's like to run a small business, they have experience in building communities, clients, corporate governance, and strategy. They don't always agree, but they are committed to the success of Clime. I learn so much from spending time with each of them and it's helping me become a more resilient CEO without losing who I am.

In terms of my leadership team, I've had the great fortune to work with amazing women over the last ten to fifteen years. I've also had a couple of great female mentors who have helped shape the way I look at recruiting talent. It was not a deliberate move to have the level of diversity we have today, but it is a deliberate strategic decision to have cultural and gender diversity across our business. We want a better representation of the community we serve; we want diversity of thinking, ideas, and opinions. To affect meaningful change in anything, you must be open to other peoples' views and experiences. I also think it's a lot easier to attract talented women when there are role models. As the expression goes, "you can't be what you can't see." We have many women in our company, and they are all different. They range in age, cultural background, experience, and industry experience. It's much easier to "see yourself" in our company when you walk in for an interview. We're a very relatable bunch of people.

How would you describe your leadership style?

My leadership style is adaptive. I spend a lot of time being curious about our industry, observing how the constituents evolve through the ecosystem. I use what I learn as an input to how I lead. There are times where I lean into my instincts and experience to make the required decisions because I know only I can or must. There are times where I consult others in my team to help shape the next move. As a CEO, the greatest skill to harness is the ability to see three steps ahead and work out the right moves. That's why we're the leaders and tasked with the responsibility of navigating uncertainty, our people, and the future of our company.

I'm learning to accept uncomfortable situations, being in environments where I'm not sure what the right course is but knowing that I have years of experience where I can use my existing capability to make a considered decision. I've also learned that a decision is not simply defined by "good or bad," it's just another way in. Making a decision is a critical part of leadership (CEO or otherwise) because it provides you with insight and information. If a decision I make is not fit for purpose, then I'll know and can adjust accordingly. Sitting on the sidelines procrastinating doesn't help anyone. It delays the inevitable or, worse still, sets a course that you may not be able to unwind.

When it comes to leading people, I love bringing out the best in their strengths and talents. All our people have completed the Clifton Strengths Finder™ to help them understand what they are naturally good at and how this can help them in their role. I've used this framework for years and it works. It allows our people to be individuals within a team. It opens access to new skills and ways of thinking without people worrying about what they're not good at. Working from strengths is a useful way of allocating resources to projects and assists with cross collaboration. It helps our people learn from each other while applying their strengths to a project or process. When we get it right, and it takes conscious practice to implement this way of being, we get momentum fast and outcomes are achieved which deliver the objective. It gets our team closer to our goal and they enjoy the process along the way. The adage "be yourself, everyone else is taken" rings true when working from strengths. Our people can remain ambitious, entrepreneurial, and competitive without worrying about being isolated or sabotaged. We can also have a lot of fun along the way. I remember when I first introduced Strengths Finder™ into Clime, there was a little bit of suspicion and cynicism about the survey. I was fortunate that many of the team members I had worked with previously encouraged everyone to do it by sharing their existing profiles and what they'd gained from the experience. We have a couple of "raving fans" who swear by it and use the insights from the report to get back on track when they are feeling off center.

Of all the leadership lessons I've learned over the years, the one that sticks with me the most is "if no one is following, then you're not leading." Understanding that leadership is a responsibility of service, under-standing, and integrity is critical in a leader. People who are following want to know they are going to be safe, respected, and valued.

How instrumental is your chair in supporting your initiatives?

John is a mentor, role model, and supporter in more ways than I expected. He creates an environment where we can have candid and robust conversations without diminishing my views or role. We don't always agree, but we are aligned in our purpose for Clime and the way we want to help our clients.

He expects the best of me and will pull me up when I've drifted from the main goal. In a small company, it's very easy to get caught up in the noise and think I'm the person who has to solve every problem that comes my way. My Chair provides coaching which helps me focus on the big rocks, spend time and energy where it's most valuable, and remove the day-to-day clutter. Having a great Chief Operating Officer has been another profound decision in my career. Kara has this way of getting stuff done quickly, and with a smile which would drive others crazy. She thrives on process and communication which is a talent much needed when we're trying to move mountains.

A respectful relationship between a chair and CEO is essential to running a successful company. The CEO is a representative of the board, and if there are opposing values or views on the direction of how the company needs to run, it can be disastrous. No one wins, or worse, the company ceases to exist. I am fortunate to be working with a Chair who believes in supporting the CEO; I've worked with many who did not. It can be exhausting running a company with multiple stakeholders, especially in a highly regulated industry like ours. The addition of subversive turmoil and dealing with competing agendas is just unnecessary. The job is difficult enough.

When it comes to designing the strategy, most of this is done with the leadership team and then discussed with the board. John is a sounding board, voice of reason, and uses his vast experience to test my thinking and hypotheses. Being naturally curious means I'm always researching our industry, parallel markets and learning from other CEOs. However, I don't get caught up too much in our competitors other than to see how they are working with clients and technology. Understanding consumers across any industry and how they behave with whatever widget or service is being sold is fundamental to building a strategy. Once I've gathered information that makes sense to me, I'll run by John to test my thinking and draw on his knowledge and hear his perspective. John sees the world in numbers, and he has a very sharp mind. He is also a big-picture thinker, a valuable asset to have at the leadership table when pitching an idea or concept. Once an idea or strategic initiative gets approved, I know it will be supported by the board and they will help remove barriers to achieve the objective. Wisdom and an open mind are worthy qualities when it comes to getting a strategic initiative approved. Thankfully, I have access to both from my board.

Was it challenging to recruit women and cultural diversity in a predominantly male industry?

Despite financial services still being very male dominated, it hasn't been challenging to recruit women or a diversity of talent into our company. I used to wonder why we attracted such a wide range of cultures and ages into our company until I looked in the mirror!

I'm a colored, 55-year-old female CEO in an industry that doesn't typically look like me. Earlier in this chapter I mentioned, "you can't be what you can't see." When I took on the role I was asked if I was the only colored female CEO in the ASX. I am not. The person I admire and who I "see" as an inspiration is Shemara Wikramanayake, CEO of Macquarie Group. She's successful, hardworking, grounded, and running one of the most respected companies in Australia. Less than a generation ago, this would have not been possible.

While I haven't tested the hypothesis, my intuition tells me the reason we are attracting women and people with diverse cultural backgrounds is because our leaders are relatable, our interview process involves many people across the business giving prospective employees an early sense of what it would be like to work here, and it has appeal. It's the same with attracting female business owners as clients. We have strong entrepreneurial female leaders. If you're a female business owner looking for a community who will help you grow and learn in a safe and supportive environment, we're the company to partner with.

Like attracts like. I remember the first time this dawned on me. I'd been speaking to a (female) adviser who was looking for a new licensee to join. Anthea and I had many phone conversations as part of our mutual fact-finding/due-diligence process. She had been referred to me by an industry peer and had conducted some background research but still had many questions. We got along well on the phone and each time we spoke there was another point of intersection – family, children, values. One day she said, "I'm coming down to meet you." She was based in Brisbane and I'm based in Sydney. It's not unusual for prospective clients to come to you, but this person had been through a tumultuous time with her previous group and I was certain she'd want us to come to her to prove we were worthy of her business. However, one morning, travel to Sydney she did, and there she was sitting across my desk grilling me with all sorts of questions about our values, approach, and beliefs about financial advice. Anthea had heard we were attracting many female business owners of various ages and stages of the business cycle, and this really appealed. At a point in the conversation, I remember saying, "I'm not sure why but we seem to be attracting some great women into this community." Anthea immediately burst out laughing… clearly, I had missed the joke… and said, "Don't you realize why?" I shook my head indicating I didn't, to which she promptly responded, "Because you are a female leader, and it shows that you can relate to us." I consider myself a relatively fast thinker with good analytical skills, but at that moment I was genuinely taken by surprise by the statement. Suffice to say, I've never taken my position as a female leader for granted and, importantly, Anthea joined our community and has become a cherished friend.

If one person can do this, others can, and this is how we create possibilities for ourselves and others. Creating an environment where all are welcome despite color, creed or gender is not only the right thing to do, but also a smart business decision. McKinsey's 2019 DEI study showed that top-quartile companies with a greater representation of diversity outperformed by 36% in profitability compared to those in the bottom quartile. The results are similar for gender diversity, and performance accelerates when there are more than 30% women in executive positions.

Despite the numbers stacking up, here we are in 2022 having the same discussions about getting women, and diversity of representation, into executive positions. Which leads me to believe there's still a wide gap between knowing and understanding or acceptance. It's one thing to know the importance of good nutrition, it can be much harder to take the necessary action to make eating better a way of life. We have a society that seems to be on a perpetual diet. Looking at this positively – it's another competitive advantage for CEOs who are prepared to sit outside of the status quo and build a company whose foundation is built on the principles of DEI. I'm very proud of the gender diversity in our company. Our board is 40% female, our leadership team is 60% female, and 41% of our employees are female. No matter the gender or cultural background, we're all proud of this.

In the past, you didn't believe in quotas but you do believe in them now, why is that?

I didn't believe in quotas. I believed if I worked hard, demonstrated I was capable, delivered results, and made it known I aspired to be an executive, that would be enough. Perhaps a rose-colored view of the corporate world coupled with the naivety that all I had to do is keep pushing through. This, mixed in with that fatal gene many women have of "imposter syndrome," held me back from trusting my instincts, standing up for myself and asking for sponsorship into the roles I knew I could do better than many of those appointed.

My mind shifted from "anti-quota" to "we need quotas" one evening when I attended an executive intensive at AGSM. I'll never forget the evening. It was about 11pm and I was sitting with four of the male lecturers and attendees. We were discussing gender diversity and I started on my soap box about being the "right person for the job" as the key criteria for promotion. By the way, I still believe this and hire accordingly. However, during this evening, one of the lecturers asked, "How do you become the 'right person' if you never get the airtime to learn, grow and develop?" The question made me sit up and listen differently. I removed my blinkers and started diving into this conversation, wanting to learn more about their views and by the end of the conversation I realized I'd been indoctrinated into a way of thinking which I thought made sense, but it didn't. I was carrying a bias which had created a blind spot. It was a turning point, and ever since I've advocated for quotas.

Put simply, if you don't have a seat at any table, how do you get a meal? We don't (didn't) invite enough women to the table, which means there are less who get the exposure and experience needed to become executives. As these women move up, they've spent so many years fighting hard to be recognized they've simply run out of steam to help others. Not because they don't want to, but because once they are in the seat, women are often still contending with "earning the right" to be there.

When I refer to quotas, I now talk about access to opportunity first and foremost. We need to get more women into the places where they can be mentored, coached, and sponsored by great executives, learning from others that have gone before them. How can we expect to increase gender diversity in leadership if the "pipeline" doesn't exist? How can we create a more inclusive workplace if our people don't identify with or aspire to be the leaders they see? Being a CEO is a skill that must be learned, and you can only do this if you are exposed to other CEOs – no matter their track record. The type of access required to become an executive can take years, and often it's because someone is in the right place at the right time. To make the changes required, we need to design the pathway and encourage women to trust they will be supported and receive the same opportunities as their male counterparts. From here it's easier to springboard into the role that best suits the capability of said person. But if women aren't anywhere near the opportunity, it becomes almost impossible to be considered for leadership roles.

I'm very thankful for that late night at AGSM, and the men who challenged my ideals. I'm more mindful of creating opportunities for everyone who's aspiring to be a leader, no matter how they identify themselves.

What would you like to see in future workplaces for your children?

We have one child who wants to be a bio-mechanical engineer and has held that goal since she was eight years old, and another still figuring it out, but he has a natural knack for leadership and inclusiveness, so I hope he forges a path into leadership no matter the industry.

I'd like to see a workplace where this type of conversation is no longer necessary, that it's a history lesson we've learned and progressed from. Why we are still discussing gender and cultural diversity in 2022 is beyond me. Australia is a multicultural society shaped by all sorts of people, and for the most part it's relatively safe to be yourself. I know there is still a group out there who create a fear-based undercurrent, whether it be race, gender or culture. But it doesn't mean we give up and accept ignorance. "The standard you walk past is the one you're prepared to accept." I hope by the time our children enter the workforce full time, ignorance and bigotry is not a standard we accept.

My all-time favorite quote is from Maya Angelou, an amazing woman, writer, and activist. She wrote, "You only are free when you realize you belong no place – you belong every place – no place at all. The price is high. The reward is great."[26] This is the future I would like to see for our children. One where they can be themselves and thrive in a place where they can belong but don't have to abandon themselves to fit in.

Why do you see yourself as an "unconventional" CEO?

I see myself more as an "unconventional leader." I don't fit the typical "family photo" which is widely common in the financial services sector. I'm female, colored, and didn't come through my career journey to CEO of a financial services company the traditional way. That's just how my life turned out. I no longer look at this as right or wrong, but I don't accept it's the only way to progress a career.

I have a strong sense of social justice and will actively speak out (sometimes it has been to my detriment) on issues that I believe need a voice. When I was younger, it impacted my career because I would pursue a cause and stand in the firing line for those who couldn't or wouldn't stand up for themselves. After many years of coaching (and therapy), I've changed the way I use my voice and for whom. I still advocate for change, but now do it in a way which removes the noise and focuses on the outcome. Most people want a greater good for society, their family, their workplace, and if a leader can use that belief and energy to galvanize others, the results can be staggering.

Before I became the CEO of Clime, I was the CEO of the company that we purchased after it was put up for sale post a parent company going into administration. It was the beginning of Covid, I'd just returned from a month away with my family and within days of being back I found myself leading a company through a sale with receivers, administrators, and lawyers at thirty paces. I was a salaried employee and could have made the decision to step away and find another role (and much less distress); instead I stayed and with the team we began to lay the course for the best possible outcomes for our clients, people, and community.

We took the road less travelled. Many of our competitors had faced similar situations and their clients found themselves left in the dark with little or no communication, and a lack of leadership direction.

Our team opened the communication, sought help from our industry partners to look out for our community and committed to finding a solution (within our control) which saw everyone arrive safely on the other side of the transaction. And we achieved it.

I wrote to our community every day from the moment the sale process commenced, up until a month or so after we found a new owner. There were 147 pieces of communication. I gave my word I would write every day even if there was nothing new to say. During this process, my father passed away and I was the executor of the estate. While I was dealing with all this entails and helping my family plan the funeral, which I ended up watching on Teams due to Covid restrictions between states, my team held the course, continued to write daily while I was out of action and led the business as we had all agreed. Their courage was extraordinary; they continued to press on despite understanding there may not be a role for them on the other side of the transaction.

We also set up an advocacy group for our clients who fielded and led conversations among themselves. The guiding principles of the group were simple: look out for the community, voice the concerns, and help find the right home. In turn, we would ensure we responded to any questions as transparently as possible. They understood some discussions were held under confidentiality agreements and could not be shared. The group did not have to divulge any of the matters discussed between themselves. We had made an agreement to stick together throughout the sale process, and work toward a common good. We all kept our promises to each other.

Does this make me unconventional? Possibly. One thing is certain, it reduced the number of sleepless nights knowing I had a community willing me to succeed, and they were right beside me every step of the way, even though the future was uncertain.

Did you see growth in financial performance with greater diversity in teams?

We saw a shift toward growth in financial performance within the first half year after my appointment. It was encouraging to see the shackles come off the team and watch them settle into doing what they do well. Once employees had certainty of who was going to lead our company, and they were supportive of the decision, the momentum shifted toward getting the job done. Performance was significant off the back of a strong financial market, and opportunities opened.

Being ASX-listed, we are highly visible. Our company had been in the media a lot, some of which was controversial. It was important to move away from that distraction and focus on looking after our clients. We couldn't control what was said in the media, but we could control where we spent our time and energy. The one-on-one conversations really assisted with the first ninety-day decisions and created the catalyst for the way forward.

This led to a successful capital-raising widely supported by our shareholders and employees, which then enabled our company to pursue several strategic opportunities and acquisitions. Many of these were identified late FY21 and early FY22, so we are in the early stages of either settling the deal or transitioning the business. All this information is publicly available.

Interestingly, each opportunity has come to us via referral from a business partner or client, which is a great endorsement of how they view our company. It's also created an implied trust with the prospective partner or business owner, making it easier for each party to be open with their expectations and ideal outcomes. The moment you can move into an authentic and transparent discussion, the easier it is to make a go/ no-go decision. If there is alignment based on similar values and growth objectives, then the deal becomes mutually beneficial. It does not mean the process to get to the finish line is without obstacles, but when all parties are working toward the same objective, getting through these obstacles benefits everyone.

These recent transactions have laid a strong platform for long-term sustainable growth, opened new markets attracting new clients, and brought in some very talented people. The building blocks to create a financially successful company. I believe our future is very bright.

Do you have a book you would recommend for CEOs to read?

There are so many books about CEO success and failure, and I've read hundreds of them. Each book has a lesson to learn, a metaphor you can relate to, and dozens of frameworks you can implement (if you can remember which book it came from).

However, there are books that have stuck with me, and I've gone back to time and time again. These are ones whose pages have yellowed, been dog-eared, have notes scribbled in the margins and colored post-it notes tagging an insight that has held over the many iterations of my career.

In no particular order, these are:

Built to last, Good to Great and *Great by Choice* by Jim Collins.[27] The stories of resilient leaders who have built sustainable companies, challenged the status quo, and led through changing market dynamics are worth reading and testing within your company. In all these books, the lesson I've taken with me in every role as a leader is, "How do the decisions I make today shape the type of company I leave behind?" If the decision does not help the future sustainability of the company, then I need to reconsider. For companies to endure, leaders must respect they are responsible not only for the decision they make today, but also for the one that may impact the company's longevity. Or, as my Chair likes to say, "Be an owner not a renter."

Who moved my cheese? by Spencer Johnson.[28] A very simple yet effective book which helps people understand how to deal with change. I bought it before jumping on a plane from Sydney to Melbourne. I had been made redundant from a large corporation post September 11 and I was taking time to consider my next move. I was in my early thirties and had always worked, so it was a daunting time. I boarded the plane full of apprehension, and by the time I landed I knew everything would turn out fine (it's a very short read). And it did. I was in Brisbane to attend an industry conference, and by the end of that week I had four interviews and one job offer. That offer put me on the path to where I am today, and the team I worked with back then have since become mentors and advisers to the companies I lead.

Braving The Wilderness by Brené Brown.[29] I have read all Brené's books and love every single one. I'm recommending this because it's where I first saw the Maya Angelou quote about belonging, which then led me to read all Maya's books, and there's a framework in it I often refer to. When I find myself questioning my ability to trust, or backing my own instincts, I refer to the BRAVING acronym which refers to the following:

- Boundaries
- Reliability
- Accountability
- Vault

- Integrity

- Non-judgment

- Generosity

My final book recommendation is *CEO Excellence: The Six Mindsets That Distinguish the Best Leaders from the Rest* by Carolyn Dewar, Scott Keller, and Vikram Malhotra.[30]

This is the only CEO book I've found that teaches you how to be a CEO. It's filled with practical ways to build a business, become the CEO most of us aspire to be and to learn from the best CEOs in the world. It's a lonely job and there aren't many people you can turn to who can help answer your questions (everyone is looking to you for the answers). It's a compelling read and should be part of every CEO's (current and aspiring) library.

What is your advice to other CEOs who are struggling to achieve diversity in their company even though they want to or need to?

My advice to CEOs is to seek help from outside sources, but this is only part of the solution to build your DEI policy and culture. An outside perspective is often valuable when you feel like it's "groundhog" day and you can't break the nexus. It's also a way of accelerating a much-needed shift in workplace environments.

My other suggestion is to learn from within. Start with understanding who's in your company and what they need to feel like a valued part of the future success of your business. One of the first things I did when I became CEO of Clime was schedule a one-one meeting with every team member. The meetings had no agenda (actual or implied). All I wanted out of the conversation was to learn and understand about the people who had been here for a while and seen more than I had. They knew where all the skeletons were, they had the scars, the success stories, and they knew our clients. I will always be grateful for the trust and vulnerability every person afforded their new CEO during these conversations. Because there was no agenda, people shared their personal history, family stories, beliefs, ideas for helping the company, and one person showed me a storybook he had written for his kids! People want to be heard, they want to know they have a voice and by giving them time to share whatever was on their mind (without fear of being judged), they opened their hearts to me. There were tears of joy and sadness, but I wouldn't swap this experience for the typical "tell me about your job" meetings that often happen in meetings like this.

I'm sharing this with you because to shift beyond the numbers into a company that embodies DEI, you need to first understand your people and why they get out of bed every day and come to work. Understanding your current culture will help inform your future culture. It will tell you whether you can implement step change or need to take baby steps. In our situation, our people were ready for step change. Your company may need to move slower so as not to overwhelm.

There are a few easy steps any CEO can take no matter what size of company.

Set the standard you want to see in your company. If you believe there's a need to build a more inclusive workplace (and who doesn't?), then walk the talk.

Start small by celebrating diversity. This could include acknowledging religious or cultural festivals. I remember one week where we had people celebrating or observing a vast range of culturally important events. We had people observing Ramadan, others celebrating Easter (Christian and Orthodox), Rama Navami, and Passover in the same few weeks. Besides the amazing food, sweets, and chocolate eggs which arrived daily, we learned a lot about traditions which are important to our people. It was fabulously rewarding to see everyone's willingness to share these traditions with each other.

Help your people understand their strengths. I've used Clifton's Strengths Finder™ for years and it works. It allows people to be confident with what they are good at and less consumed by worrying about their weaknesses. If a company wants to increase inclusivity, then leaders need to learn more about the individuals they lead and how to maximize their potential.

If employees aren't fearful about their roles because they know they are playing to their strengths, it creates space for helping and learning from others. All ships lift in a rising tide. I've used this tool for years and it works. It's helped with promotions (inside and outside the company), redefining roles, moving people to roles better suited to their strengths and talents, and has helped others self-select out of a company because we weren't the right fit. Imagine how much anxiety gets relieved when people know they are empowered to decide about their future with an outcome which works for them and the company. I've seen many "aha" moments when someone reads their report, connecting the dots on why their job is so rewarding or why it's not. Understanding your uniqueness makes it much easier to understand others.

Once you have a plan or have some evidence of the shift, share it with the board. Let them know what you're doing and why. Directors are there to help the strategic direction of your company; this includes the people component. Without good people who are committed to the flag on the hill, you can't succeed. It's good business sense to have a people strategy as powerful as your financial objectives. They go hand in glove.

Mike Bennetts, CEO, Z Energy Ltd

Mike is the founding chief executive of Z Energy Limited, the company that purchased the downstream business of Shell in New Zealand in April 2010 and Chevron in June 2016. Z listed on the NZX/ASX in August 2013 and was delisted in May 2022 when purchased by Ampol.

Mike is an internationally experienced chief executive with skills and capabilities developed within the global energy sector. His career development has included exposure to most global energy markets, with his early career development being grounded across sales, marketing, IT, and finance. From 1992 to 2008 he served in various senior leadership roles in South Africa, China, Singapore, and in the United Kingdom (at BP's global headquarters).

Mike has served as a Director of various private and public companies and joint ventures and is presently a Director of Loyalty New Zealand Limited (www. loyalty.co.nz) (since 2010) and the Chair of Punakaiki Fund Limited (https://punakaikifund.co.nz) (since 2016), a $100m investment fund that makes long-term investments into high-growth technology companies.

In 2016, Mike was awarded CEO of the Year within the Deloitte Top 200, with Z also being recognized as Company of the Year.

In 2017, Mike co-founded the Climate Leaders Coalition (https://climateleaderscoalition.org.nz) and spent five years as their Convenor.

Mike holds a Postgraduate Diploma in Corporate Management. He graduated as a Bachelor of Business Studies majoring in Management from Massey University, where he was recognized as a Massey Scholar because of his academic record.

About Z Energy Limited

Z is NZ's largest transport fuel company operating a network of fuel infrastructure and distribution activities across 330 service stations and 140 truck stops through the Z and Caltex brands. Z is one of NZ's largest retailers with 52 million transactions a year, 40% of these exclusively through Z's convenience stores where annual revenues are over $400m.

Z has a clearly stated commitment for the transition to a low-carbon future. This has resulted in investment in domestic biofuels manufacturing, a 70% share of one of NZ's independent electricity retailers (Flick – www.flickelectric.co.nz) and a 30% share of a vehicle sharing company (Mevo – https://mevo.co.nz).

Interview with Mike Bennetts

Question – Can you share with me your career journey that led you to your CEO role at Z Energy?

I originally went to university to study law, and after a year I realized it was not for me. Much to my parent's horror (as I was the first in my family to attend university), I dropped out and went contract cleaning so I could buy my first house at twenty-one. Realizing this type of work was not a long-term option, I managed to fluke an interview and secure a job with BP

New Zealand as a trainee sales rep. After a few years of that, I had a number of head-office roles around sales, marketing, strategy, and IT, across both line and project-based roles. During this time, I completed my undergraduate and then postgraduate studies while I was working full time, graduating as a Massey Scholar.

Still with BP, I took up my first international assignment in Durban, South Africa, as a Regional Sales Manager for the Natal and Transkei provinces. After a year in that role, I was moved to Johannesburg to head up the development and scaled-up rollout of BP's convenience stores and other non-fuel revenue generation like car washes.

After a few years of that, we returned to NZ so we could have our two children (two in two years!) and get ready for an extended period of time overseas as I was placed on BP's international development program. This resulted in a move to Shanghai (China) in 1998, which was one of Asia's fastest-developing cities. While there I was mostly focused on business development and then moving into strategy to support BP's ambitions to scale up in China.

My next move (1999) was to Cape Town (South Africa) as Sales and Marketing Director. This was a turnaround situation as the business unit had been one of the worst performing within BP's downstream segment. Within a year we were executing a new marketing strategy; a business model delivering a 30% reduction in costs; growth in market share against a previous three-year decline; and strong cash flow through the best debtor's performance for at least a ten-year period.

As part of the acquisition of Castrol South Africa (2000), I moved to Commercial Director within the same business unit as previously, responsible for the finance, accounting, and strategy functions, and leading the integration of the Castrol consumer and manufacturing operations into BP's portfolio.

I moved to London to BP's corporate center in 2001 as the Chief of Staff for the CEO of BP's global supply and trading business. This gave me up-close exposure to the corporate activities of one of the world's leading companies as well as working within the most entrepreneurial and least "big oil" part of the BP Group.

In 2003, I moved to Singapore as CEO for BP's Supply and Trading for the Eastern Hemisphere – a geography covering sub-Saharan Africa, the Middle East and Asia Pacific. There were ten offices across this region with twenty-five nationalities working in the Singapore regional office.

Eventually, my career with BP spanned twenty-five years, living in five countries through sixteen different roles, and exposure to all of the world's energy markets. I share with people that this enabled me to "know very little about a whole lot." I have no particular area of functional expertise (or depth) but the breadth of my career and personal development enables me to generate linkages and insights that others may not be able to.

By the end of 2008, what mattered most to me had deviated from BP's priorities, so I resigned and, as a family, we migrated back to NZ. I deliberately took a sabbatical for a minimum of six months and preferably no longer than twelve months. This gave me time to reconnect with NZ having first left seventeen years before, do some independent studying and research on organizational development (thank you internet!), and be better connected to my preferences and priorities to the extent I could be clearer on what I wanted to do for the next stage of my career.

This all came together in 2009 with an offer to be the chief executive for what became Z Energy Limited, which was formed when the New Zealand Super Fund (www.nzsuperfund.nz) and Infratil (https://infratil.com) bought the downstream assets of Shell in NZ. In 2013, Z completed an IPO (Initial Public Offer) and the two original shareholders subsequently exited the company over the following three years. In June 2016, Z bought the business of Chevron New Zealand for $785m, acquired 30% of Mevo in 2017, and 70% of Flick Electric in 2018. Z was one of New Zealand's largest public companies and ranked in the NZX20 until May 2022 when Z was delisted as it was bought by Ampol.

I was the Founding Convenor of the Climate Leaders Coalition (2017), standing down from that role in June 2022 as the Coalition moved into a new phase of development and delivery.

I have had governance roles since 1999 in joint venture, private and public companies in South Africa, China, Singapore, and New Zealand. Recent local governance experience includes NZ Refining Limited (2010–2018) and Loyalty NZ Limited (2010-present). I am currently Chair of Punakaiki Fund Limited (since 2016), and a venture capital investor ($100m FUM) in early-stage and high-growth technology companies in NZ. I am also a Chartered Member of the NZ Institute of Directors.

What inspired you to create a company with Z Energy different from other companies where you achieved gender equality in your board of directors and senior leadership team?

I recall turning up on the first day at Z, hosting a town hall with all of the employees who, until the day before, had worked for Shell, one of the world's largest companies. I introduced myself and shared some stories about my background and family. Then I stated that I was committed to Z being "a world-class Kiwi company" and showed a slide of the six elements that my independent research said were necessary to be world class. I invited people to join me on the journey to being a world-class Kiwi company, fully aware that

I knew what it was but didn't know how to get there. Contextually, by unplugging from Shell, we were like a start-up but didn't have to worry about revenues because we had already been operating in NZ as Shell for ninety-nine years. In other words, everything was up for grabs in pursuit of being a world-class Kiwi company.

A year later we respectfully retired the Shell brand and launched Z as our brand. This coincided with the launch of the Z *Why* – our statement about all that matters in Z and is the best articulation of our context. One of the opening pages says:

> "This document tells you all about what
> matters within Z. This is 'our context.'
> It applies to all of us, individually and
> collectively, all of the time. In choosing to work
> for Z, you are committing to the Z Why. 'Why'
> does not come with a straightforward answer.
> In order to help you understand the 'why,'
> we need to talk to you about our context –
> our fundamental purpose, our ambition, our
> values, our ways of working, our commitment
> to customers and workplace safety. In choosing
> to work for Z, there are things you need to
> know, things you need to do and ways you
> need to be. Most of all you need to understand
> why and wellbeing, the strategic choices, and
> so on. The Z Why does just that. At Z, we
> focus on achieving extraordinary outcomes by

setting the appropriate context, rather than by telling our people what to do. By thoroughly understanding the context, high-performing and talented people deliver better results and are more personally fulfilled."

This document has been revised three times and this is the fourth edition[31]. This document is drafted and published by myself, as editor-in-chief. This is not done by me going into a dark room, but through being informed through connecting with our people, our customers, and our other stakeholders. The challenge for me is to weave all of that diversity into a coherent context, in the same way you would weave different colors of thread into a colorful tapestry.

In essence, the inspiration came from my research while being on sabbatical, reflecting on all that I had seen go well and not so well in my global career, and weaving together the diverse perspectives of everyone around me.

How did you communicate your vision to your board of directors and team?

Our Why is the foundational document for Z, and we currently refer to the fourth edition of what was originally produced in May 2011.[32] When each edition has been updated, we engage the whole company in the contents – both what has changed and what has not changed. Prospective employees are given a copy of

Our Why at the pointy end of the recruitment process so they know exactly what they are signing up for. Once part of Z, I host a two-day induction program (called Getting Connected) which is a more in-depth conversation about the various elements of *Our Why*. This enables all of our people to be personally connected to the intersection between what matters to Z and what matters to them.

Given we have a purpose of "solving what matters for a moving world," that isn't going to be fulfilled by delivering predictable outcomes and results. For the big stuff at Z we put ourselves into the future, dream big, and then plan back from the future to the present. Put another way, we stand for things that we sometimes don't know how to deliver.

For some time now, there have been four areas where we stand for changing the game within New Zealand. These are what we call our Stands:

- Safety and Wellbeing
- Sustainability
- Community
- Diversity and Inclusion

These Stands are integrated, meaning they all work together and are of equal importance. We communicate that every person in the company is expected to behave in a way that aligns with and supports them. If our actions and behaviors in any of these are without genuine conviction, then we lack integrity and will undermine them all. They apply to all that we do with one another and our partners. Our Stand for Diversity and Inclusion can be summarized as "Being successful being ourselves and reflecting Aotearoa New Zealand."

Did you receive the support of your board of directors to implement your vision?

There has been continual support from our directors, noting they also sign up to *Our Why* when they join. Our board have been enrolled in the business case for diversity and inclusion (D&I) and, equally, it has been a close match for their own personal values. It is important to remember that diversity is a very personal thing, and people will default to their own perspective before they can engage with their company's direction and policies.

All of our strategic work around People and Culture is contained within our Organizational Development (OD) plan. Various versions of this have existed over time, and it is simply a three-year program of work, focused on what People and Culture capabilities, capacity and culture are required for Z to be able to deliver on its purpose and strategy. D&I has always been a workstream within the OD plan.

At least once a year, the board reviews progress on the OD plan, then separately and specifically on the D&I metrics and milestones. This has ensured mutual accountability and the chance to step back and consider progress in the current context and what is required for Z's ongoing success.

Z is also very transparent about its performance with D&I, both the good and the bad. This manifests in formal external reporting like the Annual Report[33] (where more data is published than what compliance calls for) through to posts on social media, like a recent one about Z's decision to pay the full employer KiwiSaver contribution for the whole of an employee's parental leave period, and part-time employees will get their KiwiSaver contribution based on the full-time salary equivalent rather than their actual pro-rata pay.[34] These two issues are far more acute for women than men.

Did you hire internal or external consultants to help develop the implementation plan?

The implementation plan (and its continued evolution) has been very much an internal endeavor. Our People and Culture team generate and manage the plan, with many of the initiatives coming from collaboration across the company – through focus groups, empathy interviews,[35] and qualitative feedback from Peakon (www.workday.com/en-us/products/employee-voice/overview.html), our monthly engagement survey.

The executive team review progress against the plan each quarter and the board once a year.

We have taken opportunities to learn from the outside by seeking external accreditation like Gender Tick (www.genderatworkcommunity.org.nz/gendertick) and Rainbow Tick (www.rainbowtick.nz). These have been invaluable in eliminating the risk of degradation or resting on our laurels. They have also exposed us to best practices across NZ and enabled us to connect with other organizations who are implementing initiatives that we are just beginning to introduce ourselves.

One of the more impactful initiatives has been the role modeling of the women on the executive team. In celebration of International Women's Day, our female executives have hosted meaningful and authentic company-wide conversations about what it is like to be a senior woman in a corporate setting. This has demonstrated their own authenticity and diversity as well as giving confidence to others deeper in the organization who are battling with the mystical goal "to have it all." Our female directors have also participated in these conversations over the years.

How long did it take to start seeing the difference in cultural change?

Like any element of culture change, there were both quick wins as well as entrenched positions. With enterprise change, it is important to give visibility to the early wins as well as what is not going well and what is going to be done about that.

One example of an early win – given the progress made in the first year, the formal Women's Network decided to disband, since all of their requests had been met and the more obviously organic and collaborative nature of the D&I agenda in Z – rather than Shell's command and control approach – supported a more informal and frequent engagement.

Over time, we have established networks for the Rainbow community, a refreshed women's network (the issues today are more systemic and complex than in the past), and, most recently, a neuro-diversity network. These are typically sponsored by one of the executives, with the work program very much in the hands of the network's community. This functions and delivers like a community of practice within an agile framework (www.scaledagileframework.com/communities-of-practice).

The regularity and transparency of reporting on our D&I metrics and milestones gave confidence to many that this was a strategic initiative that was not a one-year wonder. As we achieved success in some areas, we have continually evolved the diversity metrics and milestones to go beyond our original focus of gender and closing the obvious gaps. Achieving good gender balance at board and executive level a few years ago enabled us to go further on other systemic gender issues like pay parity, financial literacy, and the inequality in retirement funds for working women.

Did you have resistance to your vision – at the beginning and during your tenure?

As you can imagine, any time you put emphasis on one particular group of employees, say females, then some of the groups not being emphasized feel left out or marginalized. From that historic position of relative privilege, it can feel like you are losing something if someone else is prioritized to address those historical imbalances.

Our approach here has been to respectfully engage with the different and sometimes conflicting perspectives, continually listening for mutual outcomes and ways for meaningful progress. That said, when differences seem too great, we point people to our Stand for Diversity and Inclusion and remind them that the why and what are already existing commitments, and this conversation is about how we deliver on those existing commitments.[36]

How did sustainability reporting impact the operations of your company and what are your thoughts on ESG reporting?

Z has been progressive and an early adopter of many of the non-financial aspects of corporate reporting, like Integrated Reporting (www.integratedreporting.org/

resource/international-ir-framework), TCFD (www. fsb-tcfd.org), etc. These external reporting standards have helped shape both our thinking and actions, and you cannot help but be reflective for what is needed next when you are reporting on what has just been.

Being an early adopter has enabled us to generate the opportunities from this rather than feeling that we are having to comply with something forced upon us from the outside. Commitment is a far better source for change than compliance. It has also enabled us to connect with other NZ organizations who are early in their journeys so we can collectively share experiences and avoid the common pitfalls.

This approach also enabled us to realize that our Annual Report communicates with more than just our shareholders, and is meaningful for our wider stakeholder group, which includes potential employees. Being visible through our reporting is effectively like putting up the sign "open for business" and has resulted in stakeholders connecting with us and offering help and support for our journey.

What is your advice to other CEOs who are struggling to achieve diversity in their company even though they want to or need to?

For diversity, get clear on your context (ie the why for change) and what you are committed to at a point in the future, ie what you stand for with respect to diversity.

This needs to be as much about your personal stand as it is about what the company is committed to, because the CEO needs to be a visible and authentic leader on this, like any aspect of culture.

You can then contrast and compare that stand with the current reality to identify gaps and what is missing. Engage your people, including the greatest critics of those diversity gaps, to generate the actions which close the gaps. After that, it is the usual management practices of setting targets, developing plans, and reporting results. I'd also suggest you add ways in which you can capture what you are learning, as well as getting external perspectives to overcome potential blind spots.

Benn Lim, Chief Operating And Impact Officer, Arowana

Benn Lim is the Chief Operating and Impact Officer of Arowana, a global B Corporation-certified group that has a long-term commitment to building sustainable businesses that have a positive impact on economies, industries, and the people they employ. His mission is to help businesses sustainably transform and evolve to become businesses that are not only profitable but create a positive impact for people and the planet.

He led Arowana's B Corp certification, including the BIA for their operating companies VivoPower and EdventureCo. In January 2021, Arowana incorporated its Purpose and Stakeholder clause into the company's constitution following shareholder approval.

His career experience covers wealth-management and asset-allocation advice, corporate finance, investor relations, risk and governance, human resources, corporate affairs, and organizational development. He has previously worked for UBS, and Commonwealth Bank.

In 2022, he was recognized as the "Investment Firm Executive of the Year" by *CEO Monthly Magazine* in the C-suite Awards, which acknowledges the top C-level professionals who spearhead innovation, overcome challenges, and drive for distinction in their respective industries.

More importantly, he is a father to two vibrant and active boys, and in his own time he enjoys reconnecting with nature, taking bush walks, and practicing mindfulness.

About Arowana

Arowana was established in 2007 and, at its inception, Arowana operated as a Sydney-based specialist fund manager focused on Australasian investments. Since then, Arowana's strategy and model has evolved into a unique global enterprise that directly owns and operates listed and unlisted enterprises, as well as having investments in specific sectors around the world.

Today, Arowana has grown from its Australian roots into a global B Corporation with operating companies and investments in electric vehicles, renewable energy, vocational and professional education, technology and software, venture capital, and impact asset management. Our business model is simple: we directly invest in and operate impact-oriented enterprises that can be scaled globally, typically working in partnership alongside entrepreneurs and leadership teams to provide the support that is essential to realizing great success.

With decades of experience as both an investor and operator in diverse fields, and as entrepreneurs ourselves, we have the know-how to help develop, grow, and overcome inevitable challenges along the way, never losing sight of the long term.

The Arowana team today has an uncommon blend of cross-functional skills across operations, technology, and investment. We endeavor to attract and retain top talent, while embracing diversity and inclusion, and are constantly adding new expertise to create a well-rounded, agile, and future-proofed enterprise.

We value collaboration, growth, and development of our people, as we strive for excellence and respect.

Our culture does not just help attract amazing people, it amplifies our abilities and helps our employees do their best work.

To grow our companies, we must first grow our people: those who will overcome the inevitable challenges of growing a business; those who will find value-creating solutions that will contribute to our triple bottom line of people, planet, and profit.

Hence, we have carefully considered Arowana's core purpose which is to *Grow People, Companies, and Value.* This provides the foundations for our long-term commitment to build strong, sustainable businesses that will have a positive impact on economies, industries, and the people they employ.

We are also proud that Arowana has been recognized for our impact, our innovation, leadership, and execution globally with awards from Real Leaders, Fast Company's Best Workplaces for Innovators, the International Business Awards (IBA), the Asia Pacific Stevie Awards, and the Turnaround Management Association (TMA).

Incidentally, we took the name of Arowana from a tropical freshwater fish primarily found in Southeast Asia, because of its unique characteristics. The Arowana is a highly resilient and resourceful fish known for its boldness. Growing to an average of three feet in length, it can jump more than two meters out of the water to catch food. Rare in the wild, it dates from prehistoric times and is a survivor with a long history of adaptation. For us, this fish is a good metaphor for our business: resilient, resourceful, bold, and adaptable.

Interview with Benn Lim

We would love to hear about your diverse background as well as your experience.

I grew up in Kuala Lumpur, the capital city of Malaysia, in the 1980s, in a middle-class suburb. I was one of the lucky ones – my father was a scholar and in his youth was awarded a government scholarship to study abroad. He gained a Master's in Horticulture from the University of Louisiana, USA, and then a PhD from the University of Adelaide, where I was born. We eventually returned to Malaysia, where my dad became a lecturer at the Agricultural University of Malaysia.

Growing up, I lived most of my childhood naïve to the inequalities of society, but my first memory of how differently other children lived was when I was about seven or eight years old. I remember a little boy and girl around my age walking from house to house, carrying a heavy basket filled with packets of Nasi Lemak (rice cooked in coconut milk with sliced cucumbers and anchovy sambal), selling them for 30c a packet. If you have ever been to Kuala Lumpur, you will know how hot and humid it is and walking with a heavy load was not a novelty just to make some pocket money, but rather a necessity to support their family. Over the years, many children from other families would walk by our house selling food.

I was lucky enough to have been born in Adelaide, which enabled me to return to Australia after high school to go to university, where I completed my Bachelor of Economics at Sydney University. Back in Malaysia, as I was not a *bumiputra* (a Malaysian of indigenous Malay origin), I would have been subjected to the 90:10 ethnic quotas favoring *bumiputra* students, my own personal encounter of how not all things in life are equal.

After university, I started my career at Commonwealth Securities, the discount broking arm of Commonwealth Bank Australia (CBA), initially as a customer service officer. I then took on a business development role to help grow their investment advisory arm. From there, my career path progressed, and I joined the private bank division as an investment adviser. A few years later, I left CBA to join a global wealth-management group, UBS Wealth Management in Sydney, where I spent almost a decade, managing the financial investments for wealthy families.

In 2012, prior to the birth of my first child, I started to sense something was lacking in my world, despite having a good job... I was going through a mid-life crisis. When my firstborn was just twenty months old, I made the life-changing decision to take time out from the corporate world, quit my job at UBS, and become a stay-at-home dad.

During that time, I dedicated time to my child, but also to my own personal development. I read quite a few books including *The Road Less Travelled* by Morgan Scott Peck,[37] *The Monk Who Sold His Ferrari* by Robin Sharma,[38] *The Gift of Imperfection*[39] and *Daring Greatly*,[40] both by Brené Brown, *Parenting from the Inside Out* by Dan Siegel,[41] and *Parenting for a Peaceful World* by Robin Grille,[42] to name a few.

I came to the conclusion that, as a stay-at-home dad, I needed to formalize my parenting skills, so I took a few parenting courses. Yes, these courses did make me a better parent, but equally as important, a more mindful person. I eventually went on to complete a one-year certification course to become a Certified Parenting-by-Connection instructor with Hand-in-Hand Parenting, a not-for-profit B Corp based in Palo Alto. I became the only male Parenting-by-Connection instructor in Australia, and one of a few in the world, and started to run workshops – I have been running a father's group ever since. I figured, if there was one way to help change society, it would be through the next generation. I gravitated to this approach as recent research shows that, regardless of background, a close parent-child connection throughout childhood and beyond is the strongest factor in preventing a variety of health and social problems, including young people's involvement in drugs, violence, and unintended pregnancies.

Please share your background story on how you came to work for Arowana and focused on being B Corp.

My career break gave me the opportunity to reconnect with myself from the inside out, and to reflect and visualize the future that I wanted for my family and me. When it came to my career, I did not want to be just another cog in the wheel. I wanted to be with a company where I could make a difference, a company that I could help become an example of conscious capitalism.

At first, I was at a loss as to where I could find such a company. My whole life had been spent running the spinning wheels within institutions, from university to the Commonwealth Bank and then UBS. I was also very hesitant to go back into the money-making world.

My view, however, expanded after listening to Tami Simon, the Founder of Sounds True, talk about her multiple bottom lines at Sounds True. Sounds True is the world's largest living library of transformational teachings that support and accelerate spiritual awakening and personal transformation. Their first bottom line was to be true to their mission to disseminate spiritual wisdom through books, audio, video, and events. Their second bottom line was ensuring that their workplace culture and processes embodied and reflected the wisdom of the spiritual teachings that they were offering. Their third bottom line was to ensure they were profitable, because that is the oxygen that fills the system that allows them to continue to fulfill the first two bottom lines.

In my reflection, Arowana came to mind. When I was working at UBS, I was introduced to Kevin Chin, Founder and CEO of Arowana, by a colleague. I got to learn more about Arowana and became an investor in Arowana's first fund. I followed their progress and always found what they did in business interesting as they were hands-on operators.

Kevin and I kept in touch even when I left UBS to take time out, and we discussed over coffee if there was an opportunity for me to help Arowana. Given my hesitation to jump right back into the money-making world, I was sure to ask Kevin about his views on "Money." Those who know Kevin will know that he loves Bruce Lee; his answer to me was, "My view on money is like the Bruce Lee saying, 'Be Like Water'." He elaborated, "Money, like water, is energy and helps life grow, you need to keep it flowing, if you dam it up or hoard it, it will create immense pressure and corrode you."[43] I could tell he meant what he said, that is how I ended up at Arowana.

I recall it was sometime during the winter of 2016. I was in one of my first meetings with all the other directors and I asked Kevin, "Why do we do what we do? Is it just for profit?" Kevin responded, "We grow people, grow companies, and grow value."

A few months later, Kevin asked me if I had heard of B Corporations. I had not, but Kevin attended a conference in September 2016 and walked into a session about B Corps and left convinced that B Corps would become a gold standard certification and that the ethos of B Corps aligned with our core values. Kevin asked if I would drive our B Corp certification and I gladly accepted, not realizing the demands of the challenge, but was inspired given the B Corp focus on a triple bottom line of people, planet, and profit.

In 2018, Arowana became a certified B Corporation with an initial score of 84.2 and I am happy to say that, in 2022, Arowana successfully recertified as a B Corporation and improved our impact score significantly, achieving a score of 138.8.

What makes the B Corp certification process important for achieving gender equality in senior leadership?

I recall in my younger CBA days, one of my bosses was preparing a workshop for the team and asked me, "What do you want to know?" I said to him, "I don't know what I don't know." Hence, for me, having a framework that enables me to formalize my understanding as well as to identify where more learning is required is essential.

The B Corp certification process in the first instance is a corporate awakening moment to see how much we do or do not do, and then we can start to fill in the gaps. Like all awakening moments, when we discover a better way of being, that is when our journey begins.

All companies who are committed to becoming a certified B Corp need to go through the B Impact Assessment (BIA). The BIA focuses on five key areas of impact, which are Governance, Workers, Community, Environment, and Customers, and brings to light questions within that need to be considered, some known, some not, and some that should have been known.

The BIA reviews our diversity, equity, and inclusion within the Community area of impact by assessing if the company is led by individuals from underrepresented groups; what practices the company has in place around diversity, equity, and inclusion; what diversity metrics we track; the number of women; the number of managers that are women or from an underrepresented social group; and the number of board directors that are women.

How supportive were your CEO and board of directors regarding your goals in achieving impact?

Kevin, our Founder and CEO, wanted to effect a major cultural transformation within Arowana to align with our core purpose of building sustainable companies. There were no questions about it, this was the path we were going to take, however had it been a different board or CEO it may have taken a bit more convincing.

Attaining B Corp certification is a change-management process that requires stakeholder management as well as buy-in, and if anyone reading this needs help, you do not have to look too far. We are happy to help, and there is a lot of great data demonstrating the benefits of diversity, equity, and inclusion to help the cause.

How did the initiatives translate to achieving gender equality on the board and in the senior leadership team?

We could see a gap in our board of directors – it needed someone who had commercial experience with a legal background. In addition, despite having directors from underrepresented backgrounds, there was no female board director. In the second half of 2020, when things settled down post the initial Covid lockdowns, I started searching for candidates to fill the gap on our board and was fortunate to have found Claire Bibby, who joined the board in February 2021.

Claire has been recognized as one of Australia's best lawyers, mentors, and female executives. She is passionate about mentoring the next generation of female leaders and is a mentor for Layne Beachley's Aim for the Stars Foundation.

Importantly, to enable a diverse and inclusive team, we reviewed our parental leave policies to ensure that primary carers were able to access paid and unpaid parental leave. Where employees were not eligible to receive the government-funded leave, the company would ensure the employee received full pay for the first twelve weeks of their parental leave.

The other consideration was work-flexibility requirements. Fortunately, Chandan, our Head of IT, moved us into the cloud in 2016, which enabled the team to work from anywhere. At the time, my second child was still less than a year old and I certainly appreciated the ability to have this flexible work arrangement. Rather than presenteeism at the office, our mindset is about getting the job done with no negative impact on our colleagues. I believe that, post the pandemic, this has now become the norm for most companies; a blessing in disguise for working parents.

I am happy to say our team is truly global, where it is common to have project team members working across different time zones. As Simon Sinek highlights, "Each of us has blinders. We can only see things from our own perspective. But when we come together with a common cause or a shared vision, our view broadens, and we can see and recognize things that we never could have seen on our own. That is why the best companies are diverse: they have diverse thinking."[44]

You love reading – please share the insights of books regarding diversity and business as well their benefits.

Culture Code by Daniel Coyle offers some insight into building a successful team culture.[45]

Daniel Coyle's research found that the culture of some of the world's most successful businesses, sporting teams, military units, and gangs of thieves were not just fate but created from a specific set of skills. These skills, which tap into the power of our social brains, create interactions that become a company's culture. Group culture is one of the most powerful forces on the planet; we sense its presence inside successful businesses, championship teams, and thriving families, and we sense when it is absent or toxic.

Companies who have top-performing cultures have firstly built the foundations of safety and connection to foster belonging and identity, and once these foundations are established, only then can we feel safe enough to share vulnerability and build trust among the team. At the pinnacle of these two building blocks is establishing purpose, the beacon that guides the team to their goal.

Focusing on the core foundation of building safety, Coyle demonstrates this with the "spaghetti tower challenge" between a group of MBA students and a group of kindergarten students to see which group can build the tallest spaghetti tower. The MBA students got straight to work: brainstormed ideas, were professional, rational, intelligent, organized, and their interactions were smooth. The kindergarten students, however, did not strategize, analyze, or share ideas, no questions were asked, or options proposed, hardly anyone spoke, they stood side-by-side, but their interactions were abrupt, and they would grab materials from one another.

After dozens of trials, the results showed that the kindergarten students built structures that averaged 26 inches tall while the MBAs built structures that averaged 20 inches tall.

The findings showed that, while the MBA students appeared to be collaborating, they were in fact engaged in a process called "status management" and were too worried about who was in charge, being criticized, or what the rules were.

The kindergartners, on the other hand, while appearing disorganized on the surface, were being efficient and effective, not competing for status but rather working energetically together, moving quickly, experimenting, taking risks, and noticing outcomes which helped them work toward effective solutions.

The kindergarteners succeed not because they are smarter, but because they are able to bypass the status-management process and jump in straight away, working toward their goal and performing far more effectively.

Another insight that is connected to this status-management process was from a documentary I watched called *The Mask You Live In* by Jennifer Siebel Newsom[46] (who also made *Miss Representation*, a documentary on how the media underrepresented women in positions of power). *The Mask You Live In* shines the spotlight on how early development of certain outdated and harmful notions of masculinity in boys, such as to "toughen up," is meant to emulate what it is to "be a man" and has led to a distorted sense of ego in males.

A particular insight in the documentary that stuck with me was from Dr Judy Chu, a PhD in Human Development and Psychology from Harvard University who is the author of *When Boys Become Boys*.[47] She studied a group of boys from pre-kindergarten through to first grade over a two-year period, and one of the things that came up in her study was the "Mean Team," a boys club created by the boys for the boys for the purpose of acting against the girls. In the pre-kindergarten class, there was a bit of inter-mixing early in the year but by the end of the year a boy versus girl dynamic began to emerge. Within the boy's club, a hierarchy also became clear, with rules on how things had to be. One of the rules was that the boys could not play with the girls, and if you broke that rule you would be kicked out of the club, and technically not be a boy anymore. This was the consequence for their status among the boys.

The young boys in the club feared speaking up against the dominant male for fear of being reprimanded. While not quite the same scenario as the MBA students, there is this sense of fear to maintain a status within this group of children and a group-think phenomenon also begins to form.

When I worked in banking, there certainly was a boy's club, and indeed the culture reflected the old notions of masculinity. Hence why it was important for me to learn how to be a parent and do my own personal work given now that I have two boys to raise, and to hope that the future generation can do it differently.

As Daniel Coyle highlights, the most important step is building the foundations of safety, only then can your team feel safe to share ideas. Without it, attempting to attract diversity among your talent pool will be futile.

In addition, another insight from the documentary was how society has delineated human attributes between masculine and feminine, forming gender stereotypes that somehow makes us lose our perspective of diversity and equality. Unfortunately, gender-neutral rearing appears to be harder as we are becoming much more bifurcated in terms of hyper-masculinity and hyper-femininity. Girls' products have become more pink, and boys' products have become much more camo and violent. It is not just in the toys but it's also in television programming and movies. This hyper-masculinization and hyper-feminization reflects the fact that gender is socially constructed, and we respond in ways to try to organize and simplify the world that actually end up simplifying it to such a great extent that it puts pressure on young men and young women to fit into preconceived and limiting boxes.

One of your favorite books – *Exponential Organizations* – talks about how diverse thinking can grow business exponentially by ten times; can you share your experience on this?

A book on Arowana's recommended reading list is *Exponential Organizations (ExO)* by Salim Ismail, who is the founding Executive Director of Singularity University and a serial entrepreneur.[48] One of the many steps to building exponential organizations is the team composition, where diversity is an important part of the package and particularly so for community-driven companies. Furthermore, to deliver diverse backgrounds, independent thought, and complementary skills, roles such as the visionary/dreamer, user experience design, programming/engineer, and the finance/business roles are critical in ExO teams.

This makes a lot of sense, because tackling problems requires creativity and innovation, which can only come when we have different perspectives from a diverse group of unique individuals from different backgrounds.

One great example is our education business, EdventureCo. We own DDLS, a leading Information, Communication and Technology (ICT) training business. Within DDLS, we developed a new brand called the Australian Institute of ICT (AIICT) to bring world-leading technology companies and expert instructors together to deliver industry-recognized qualifications in a flexible, blended-training format. This project was led by our Digital Transformation Director, Stacey Jacobs.

Courses are taught online by real-world professionals who share their practical industry knowledge to help students enter the ICT industry and connect with employers through our Industry Partnership Program.

In 2021, capitalizing on a gap in the market, AIICT rapidly launched ten new high-tech, high-demand IT courses, to meet the changing needs of the Australian IT industry. They brought together the world's leading technology vendors with the world's leading content providers such as Microsoft, Amazon Web

Services (AWS), CompTIA, DevOps Institute, Digital Marketing Institute, Python Institute, Pluralsight, and LinkedIn Learning, to name a few. These courses were a mix of both nationally accredited qualifications and vendor-certified accreditation bootcamps in cyber security, cloud computing, AI, growth marketing, and DevOps, which are the three most "challenging areas" for finding qualified talent in Asia Pacific, as outlined in the 2020 IT Skills and Salary report.

This resulted in AIICT growing its revenue by 579% compared to the previous corresponding period.

What is your long-term goal in achieving impact?

Personally, my long-term goal in achieving impact comes from me being a father and being there for my two sons, to guide them as best as I can from the insights that I have uncovered from my own personal journey. This, along with being a leader in my community of fathers to support one another as we all face the challenges of raising our children together.

As for my career, to achieve Arowana's long-term commitment to building sustainable businesses that have a positive impact, how I see us doing this is three-fold: first, we seek to partner with founders and companies who are looking to deliver outcomes that help society and the environment; second, we will work with them to build the processes and systems within their business model that align with our B Corp values;

and finally, we need to ensure they are sustainable in their own right, even after we are no longer investors or operators in the business.

All Arowana's portfolio companies where we have majority control are required to undertake the B Impact Assessment, and we strongly advocate for all companies where we hold a minority interest to undertake BIA as well. We also have our in-house B Corp Consultant who can assist our portfolio companies through this rigorous process.

What is your advice to other CEOs who are struggling to achieve diversity in their company even though they want to or need to?

I have led Arowana and our group companies through the B Corp certification process and have undertaken the BIA several times now. While diversity, equity, and inclusion are metrics that are measured within the assessment, diversity is not something you tick off a compliance checklist, nor is it something that you can just impose.

Creating awareness and setting targets is a good start but it requires more than that. We need to build alignment across culture, processes, and systems within the organization to ensure it is sustainable and, importantly, we need to be pragmatic. Having quotas alone does not solve the problem. Without the correct alignment across all aspects of the business, businesses can fall into the trap of looking good on paper, but actually this could lead to the risk of "diversity washing." Having team members who end up being the token diversity hire will only lead to further toxicity in the culture without actually gaining the real benefits of performance from having diverse perspectives.

Hence, we need to take a broader view to see if our business model is pro-diversity, including governance, culture, policies, systems, etc. If these are not pro-diversity, then, I think, even if we try to force diversity, we may just be setting our teams up to fail.

Working through this is a change-management project; it is not glamorous. As a COO, people expect you to ensure everything to be perfect and run smoothly... and so it should be. But be assured, if you have a great diversity process and framework you will never hear how good it is, but if you get it wrong, you will certainly hear about it!

Hence, before you try to change manage others, make sure you establish your purpose first; this will certainly help you push through in those tough moments.

As Martin Luther King so famously said in his speech, "I have a dream... that all humans are created equal... I have a dream that my four little children will... not be judged by the color of their skin [or gender or race or etc] but by the content of their character."[49]

Judith Mitchell, CEO, Next Science Limited (ASX:NSX)

Judith Mitchell originally trained in business administration and has had the privilege of always working in businesses that serve the medical community with technology. Judith started her healthcare career in administration in GE Medical, in a position that would now be considered an executive assistant role.

She worked her way up through sales and contract administration, ultrasound sales specialist, imaging sales specialist, national sales management, and then Managing Director. She spent fifteen years at GE and she believes that she learned something new every day about doing business and managing people.

She then was part of a start-up that failed. When she looked at what went wrong, she realized that she didn't understand product development well, nor did she understand what it took to get a product ready for market. In 1999, she joined Cochlear, where she spent five great years learning both product development processes and manufacturing controls. Cochlear was also her first global role and she got to appreciate the differences in the way the countries around the world did business. In 2004, she joined Synthes, and in 2007 was named the President for Asia Pacific. During this time, Synthes built a team with a reputation for outstanding service across Asia. The region spanned New Zealand to India.

In 2012, Synthes was acquired by Johnson and Johnson, and she took up the role of President, DePuy Synthes Asia Pacific, where the new challenge was about building a united team, from two teams who previously competed. In 2017, having retired from Johnson and Johnson, she took up the CEO position at Next Science and took on the whole new challenge of building a company from a great idea.

About Next Science Limited

Next Science is a fledgling company about to really spread its wings. Like all disruptive medical technologies that drive change, acceptance takes a while. We have answers to the problems caused by biofilms. These answers are safe, are not drugs, so they don't drive antimicrobial resistance, and are quite affordable. We are just building the cache of clinical evidence that will allow us to move to mainstream standards of care as a prophylactic wash in surgical procedures, where we can do the most good and directly impact the health outcomes of millions, while at the same time taking down the cost of healthcare by reducing the complications caused by infections.

Interview with Judith Mitchell

You have had a fantastic executive career over the last forty years while raising your son as a single mum, how did you achieve it?

I am very grateful for the opportunities I was given. It never occurred to me that I was driving for career success, I was just focused on driving for business success. Without question, my son is the best thing I have ever done for society – and given that in his professional life, his job as a pediatric oncologist is to save other people's children, I am always humbled by what he does on a daily basis.

When I look back, I start realizing where and when I built the knowledge that moved me through my career. I was always curious and asked my colleagues about their positions and how their responsibilities worked, so I had an appreciation of other people's challenges. I read a lot of management books, but also books on innovation and discovery. Nowadays it's podcasts, but personally I am not a very auditory learner, so for me it has always been books, and I have read hundreds of books over the years.

About twenty years ago, a colleague who is still a very close friend started to teach me neural linguistic programming. This, along with all of the various management programs of the times (Gallop, MBTI, DiSC), was really useful in showing up my weaknesses. The value of these tools is the very bright mirror that can shine in your face, so that you can see what it is you don't like in yourself and develop a pathway to change. They can also show you why you might conflict with others, which gives you a better understanding of others and better tools to manage the conflict.

The consistent foundation has to be your values and I have held the same business values throughout my career. My first business mentor would recite to me constantly, "You take care of the customers, your business will take care of itself." As I moved through management, my values became streamlined to a hierarchy in which customers come first, then staff (as they take care of the customers), and then the company. I have used this formula consistently and it is the consistency that is the key.

When people bring you a problem, they really want a consistent response. It is one of the characteristics in managers I think we all appreciate – predictability. As a manager, I needed to stand for a set of values and make my decisions according to those values. Once this is transparent, you can start to build trust and it needs to be transparent to your staff, so they can understand why you made the decision you did and learn from your experience, if only second hand.

If you have the benefit of having a senior team of managers with broad experience, then you can make the decision together. To make a business more family friendly, I encourage people to put their families before their positions. Whether it is a family crisis, or a child's school celebration, these individual occasions are responsible for the fabric of family life and missing them is like missing a stitch in knitting – you will see the hole. For me, the most memorable message at my executive training after I joined Johnson and Johnson was when the CEO said, "You can be replaced in a meeting – you can't be replaced in a meeting at home; don't ignore your families."

I do believe that business can be flexible enough for both men and women to operate in a family-friendly way and allow people the time when it is needed, and

I have always made it a point at company celebrations to thank the partners and families of the employees, as they are part and parcel of our success, for without their support for the employees, the company would have suffered.

The other lesson that decades of management have taught me is that your staff know what (and who) is working and what isn't. Leaving issues doesn't help. One of my senior staff members always reminds people that bad news doesn't age well, and as a leader we need to remember neither does bad performance. Those people that don't fit in the business, the square peg in the round hole, your people know who they are, and they are waiting for us to do something about it, so I have learned not to wait. We have all made hiring mistakes. We need to acknowledge that fit is more than skills and experience; it is also matching culture and values, and that can be missed in the interview process. We need to take responsibility for the mistake and correct it. Ultimately, mismatches don't help the employee or the company.

What were your professional experiences with women in Asian countries?

So much talent available! I have had the pleasure of working with outstanding women leaders throughout Asia. Some of their struggles are much harder than mine ever were – basically, not all of Asia is set up for women to work, the childcare infrastructure is just not there. You cannot give 110% to your work if you are worrying about your child's safety. I was also blessed with great childcare and wonderful support from my family.

In a male-dominated industry, what strategies did you put in place to employ more women?

Firstly, make them welcome, acknowledge it can be a boy's club, but don't promote the boy's club behavior. For example, make sure your "bonding session activities" suit everyone.

One that always worked well was cooking school. It is easier to pull down the barriers when people are preparing food and then eating the fruits of their labor together. It can also allow you to give people a wide cultural view when you link cuisine to culture. Over the years, I have found that teams of men and women from different backgrounds and different experiences give you access to a wider breadth and depth of ideas. This ultimately allows the team to be stronger and more resilient.

If you look at Darwinism, it isn't the strongest that survive, it is actually the most flexible, and given our life experiences, where generally it is up to the woman to manage the house, the children, and, at times, the care of the elder relatives, as well as work, women have a lot more practice at playing down any drama, troubleshooting early, and being more flexible. People call it multi-tasking, but actually it is juggling, and being able to effectively switch quickly between tasks.

What are the main differences you have seen in opportunities for women to be in senior leadership teams and in board roles over the last forty years?

Slowly but surely, women are increasing in all ranks, as are the other types of diversity in the community. Our children do not see gender or race, they see capability. As the world is a village and more and more global experiences are had, then more and more diversity will occur. As more and more companies show results that are better than average by having a diverse leadership team and diverse boards of directors, then this will continue to spur the growth. Plus, more women are coming through management, and greater flexibility in the workplace has meant there are many more women getting senior management experience and being ready to take on executive and board responsibilities.

Two things still remain the same though. We as women are typically harder on ourselves than men are. Hopefully over time, this will continue to improve. The other noticeable issue is that women in societies where mothers and sisters have not worked find it harder to bridge the gap into leadership roles. Male leaders, whose mothers and wives never worked, often struggle to manage strong, ambitious women; you need to help them so that the strong, female leaders being managed by them get the opportunities and experiences they need. Ultimately, there is no single answer as the unique nature of humans means every situation will have its own unique twist.

What is your leadership style? What typical advice do you give to your team members?

I try very hard to be a servant leader. I will consciously ask my management team, "What can I do to help you?", as I believe the role of senior leadership is to help your people achieve the agreed goal (not just measure it). How do you help? You remove the barriers, you facilitate the conflicts, you drive the agreements, and, sometimes, you are just the bad guy in the room, so they can all get together, blame you for the decision they don't like, but move on.

People often quote, "treat people the way you want to be treated." I don't think that is correct; I think it is more effective to "treat people the way they want to be treated." You are managing a group of different people who have different communication styles, different learning styles, and different values. Yes, you can align the values, but to get the best out of each individual you need to match their communication and learning needs and adapt your style.

The first piece of advice I give to leaders is, when they are making a request of their people, remember to say *why*. Without the why, this is an order not a request; without a why, people don't necessarily see or understand the context; and without the why, how do they link the request to the mission as the links are not always clear? I remember once sitting on a plane as it landed in LAX, and like most planes it was running late. There had been a medical emergency on the plane, and they needed to get the EMTs on board but the aisle was full of passengers trying to jockey to get out. The flight attendant asked twice for people to remain seated but the aisle was still packed – and to be fair the rest of the passengers could not see the EMTs at the front of the plane. I said to the attendant – tell them why you need them to sit down – and immediately after the announcement the aisle cleared.

We have a belief in Next Science – if we all know the why around the actions, we will all make aligned decisions.

What is your vision for Next Science?

Next Science is a company that has the ability to advance human health in so many areas because we meet unmet needs. So many types of chronic conditions are now accepted; people suffer, people die, and costs escalate, all because the world has not had an answer for biofilms. One such area is chronic wounds, where the cause of the chronic nature is a biofilm protecting the infection in the wound and preventing it from healing. Chronic wounds have a higher mortality rate than any cancers at this time, and higher than cardiac arrests, yet there has been no real improvement in the outcomes, and as diabetes is on the increase in most societies, so is the number of people suffering from chronic wounds. We have the technology that can change that trajectory, and at the same time it will reduce the ever-increasing cost burden to healthcare.

While it is taking us time to get our message out there, we will soon cross 500,000 patients that we have helped and that will go up exponentially as our distribution broadens and product lines increase. Our mission is to heal people to save lives, and as one of our wonderful key opinion leaders reminds me, you do that one patient and one physician at a time, and, ultimately, we will get there.

What is your advice to other CEOs who are struggling to achieve diversity in their company even though they want to or need to?

I guess my first suggestion would be to grab a mirror. What about you is stopping the progress to hire diverse candidates? Does the world think you "like hire"? To get into your company, do people need to look, act, and think like you or some of your leadership team? Do people think your work environment is intolerant of diversity, or not family friendly? Is your industry tilted toward a specific gender or ethnicity and you are going along with the tide?

You need to lead from the front, and for your next hire you need to actively recruit the best diverse candidate you can find (if two candidates are equal, then take the diverse candidate – the diverse thinking that will suddenly appear in your management meetings will be worth it). People follow their manager; the values and actions that you set as the leader of the organization are the values and actions your people will display. Once you are recruiting diverse candidates, then you can push your managers for a broader range of candidates, and also change your external recruiters (if you use them) with specific instructions to bring you diverse candidates.

Andrew Cole, Managing Director and CEO, OZ Minerals Limited (ASX:OZL)

Andrew has thirty years' experience in exploration and operations in the resources industry. Following exploration geoscientist roles in Australia, Canada, the USA, and Mexico with Rio Tinto Exploration (CRA and Kennecott), Andrew spent ten years in mine development and mine operations with Rio Tinto in Australia, China, Canada, and the United Kingdom.

He has been CEO of OZ Minerals for the past eight years. Over this period, the company has grown from one operating mine to three – two in South Australia and a mining hub in the Carajás in Brazil.

Andrew is committed to creating value and building strong relationships with all stakeholders. He is passionate about purpose and considers the culture the team is building at OZ Minerals to be its IP and competitive advantage, which empowers its people to do great things and enables OZ Minerals to be a modern mining company.

About OZ Minerals Limited

At OZ Minerals we strive to be modern. We're guided by our purpose: "Going beyond what's possible to make lives better." We believe that only when we create value for all our stakeholders will we be successful and sustainable.

Our framework of systems and behaviors, which we call The OZWay, guides us while giving us the freedom and pathways to achieve our aspirations and purpose. We are passionate about creating an inclusive culture where everyone can challenge, innovate, learn, and grow together.

We seek to have a net-zero impact on the environment as we ethically and responsibly explore, mine, and sell modern minerals. In doing so, we are contributing to a low-carbon future and economic wellbeing which, in turn, helps us achieve our purpose and contribute to a better future.

Interview with Andrew Cole

It is not often you hear a mining company focuses on being purpose-driven. Could you share how this journey started with OZ Minerals eight years ago when you were appointed as their CEO?

My wife and I were born in Perth, and back then we hadn't spent a lot of time living at home, with one son born in Australia, one in Canada, and one in the US. My career to that point had taken me to quite a few different countries, so when I was appointed as MD and CEO of OZ Minerals, I was very glad to be home in Australia.

I was excited to join OZ Minerals, as the "modern mining company" culture and values OZ Minerals had articulated were unique and highly motivating. I remember thinking at the time that OZ Minerals has so much potential: it had an enviable position with no debt and a healthy balance sheet with a fantastic set of assets, in both Prominent Hill and Carrapateena, which was an early idea then, emerging resources in Khamsin and Fremantle Doctor, and an appetite for further developing the business through exploration, business development, and the use of technology.

Once I joined, I found the people working for OZ Minerals to be very capable, passionate, and energetic. These, when combined, confirmed for me that OZ Minerals had many options going forward, and I had joined at an exciting and important time for the company.

One of the earliest things I progressed at OZ Minerals was to start a strategic planning process that drew on perspectives from across the business. It was very important to continually reflect and re-examine what a company does well and where the opportunities are, in order to continually improve and be successful. This was no different for OZ Minerals, especially as we were working toward the end of the Prominent Hill open pit in just a few years' time at that point.

So, in my first few months at OZ Minerals, I spent a lot of time listening to our people and stakeholders through a series of workshops and strategic goal-setting sessions. This helped me look at our strategy from every angle and within every discipline.

It was also important for me to make the process as transparent and collaborative as possible, so I had prioritized and committed to providing regular communications on progress via the OZ Minerals leadership team. To help me close the loop, I also asked for input and discussion across the company about where we were heading and why we did what we do every day. I encouraged each member of the OZ Minerals team to ask questions of their leaders and myself, because everyone at OZ Minerals should take an interest in our work, how we do it, what value we were creating, and why we exist as a company – this isn't something that is dictated top down; it has to be a felt experience and have belief sitting behind it.

Fast forward to today and we have a clear purpose – going beyond what's possible to make lives better – that has been jointly created by the board, our executives, our leaders, and people from across our business. It's more than a tagline, and shows how we intend to evolve and be a part of something greater than ourselves; to achieve amazing things for the good of the people we meet and society more broadly.

You have an amazing range of diversity in your company such as indigenous team members in addition to team members with cultural and gender diversity. How did you tackle the various differences in order to achieve inclusion?

Thank you for the kind comment. I think it's important to note that we're very much still on a journey with inclusion and diversity (I&D) at OZ Mineral, and I don't think we can claim to have "achieved inclusion" just yet.

I&D is not a simple thing – it's complex and multifaceted – but it is such a critical enabler for culture, which for us is what we consider to be our intellectual property. There is a desire across the business to build a progressive culture, so we embody a modern mining company that has value creation at the center of all we do. Consistent with this, we have also taken a culture-focused approach to I&D, as opposed to the industry's more traditional focus on compliance.

I think taking a culture-focused approach makes the programs more authentic, more sustainable, and more likely to succeed. That's not to say we completely ignore compliance, but we need to get ahead of compliance and create our own agenda that respects stakeholder expectations.

A long-term view needs to be taken because this work is complex; everything takes time if we want to really do it well and make sure there's a sustainable impact.

In the past, we took a more traditional approach to I&D. We looked at diversity through a female and First Nations lens, and set targets around participation, which is quite characteristic of our industry. While this helped us create some important headway and establish some powerful symbols for our company, we soon recognized this approach wasn't going to drive the long term, sustainable changes we were after, and it wasn't going to get the best out of our people either.

As a business, we often talk about coping with ambiguity and dealing with polarities. It's the same with I&D. Setting targets can be really motivating in the short term but they will only get you so far, particularly if they're done in isolation from other behavioral and culture work.

So, our emphasis had been to focus time and effort on building the foundations that will support an inclusive and diverse culture – and this is much harder and it takes more time – but we believe it will last longer; it will be more authentic and it will support people to engage and really be part of OZ Minerals. To come to work as whole people, where they can be the best that they can be for themselves, their families, and their communities.

Do you have intrinsic personal beliefs and values that you feel are aligned with the company?

I'm passionate about people, purpose, and culture, and a lot of what I do at work and outside of work is driven by a desire to use what I do, where I can, to make the world a better place. Fortuitously, this is in alignment with OZ Minerals' purpose of "Going beyond what's possible to make lives better," its How We Work Together (HWWT) principles, and its strategy – whether by design or coincidence.

Your focus on being a purpose-driven company has led to achieving gender equality in senior leadership. Why do you think this happened?

Again, we're not resting on our laurels, and we're still trying to get better at it. Businesses are made up of people like you and me, and we all have things that matter to us in addition to our jobs. When we were going through the process of articulating OZ Minerals' purpose, we asked ourselves: what's that special "something" that makes us who we are, why we like being at OZ Minerals, and what helps us connect to our personal why? The outcome of that is our purpose statement that reflects a higher order, the "why we get out of bed each day" that helps define OZ Minerals and everyone who is part of our business.

Because OZ Minerals' purpose was jointly created by the board, executives, company-wide leadership, and people from across our business, it became something that resonated with our people and helped to bring meaning and real direction to our work.

We have also consciously taken steps to sharpen our focus on improving gender equality and inclusivity in our workforce and leadership over the last year and a half through a series of system changes. I won't go through all of them, but some examples are:

- Disbanding our Executive Committee (ExCo) as a decision-making body and implementing systematized Corporate Teams sponsored by Executive Leads in its place, to reduce hierarchy and promote greater empowerment, inclusion, and diversity of thought.

- Committing to a 40:40:20 target across our Board and Executive Team aligned to best practice, and reorganized and recruited to achieve a current 47/53 (female/male) gender balance.

- Systematizing the use of Agile goal-setting and reviews, frequent team reflections, and real-time peer reviews to create less command and control and more transparency on behaviors.

- Systematizing the use of Stakeholder Teams, which draw on a cross section of the workforce (employees and contractors) and which require mandatory external representation to create greater inclusion of different perspectives.

- Reviewing our Building a Workforce and Organizational Capability Process Standards to counteract the risk of unconscious biases in talent decisions.

- Systematizing our How We Work Together principles and a more developmental focus into our culture.

- Undertaking a review to achieve gender pay equity at pay level as part of our 2021 annual remuneration review, reducing the gap from 2.3% to 0.7% for our Australian employees (encompassing all employees, not just those in "like for like" roles) and updated controls to systematize gender pay equity across the employee lifecycle (hiring, salary review, promotions etc).

- Continuing to mainstream flexible work through Work Life Plans for our workforce (to support both men and women to balance work and personal commitments).

- Updating our I&D statement to reflect a zero-tolerance approach to harassment.

What is the advice you have for your children and what type of world would you like to see them being part of?

The kind of world I would like to see my children being part of is the reason why I do the work I do. I want them to be part of a sustainable, healthy world that is full of opportunities so they can be happy, pursue what they are passionate about, and, in turn, contribute to creating a better society.

I know this is a bit ironic as mining, and miners, are perceived to be responsible for environmental damage. Some are and do, but similarly, there are many others who understand that the potential for making a huge impact can be either a positive or negative.

I'm fortunate to be in the position I'm in, in the company I'm in – one that is focused on modern minerals that are essential for a decarbonizing world. Electric vehicles, renewable energy systems that generate power from solar, hydro, thermal, and wind energy across the world, all need copper as a conduit. And I am glad to be part of the system of enablers for this change.

The most important advice for my children is to focus on what's important as a priority, always, and never compromise it. Unfortunately for most of us it's a lesson we learn the hard way. Connected and caring family, personal physical and mental health, and happiness driven by what you do for yourself and what you equally do for others – these, if stable and maintained, provide the foundation for all else.

You have grown your company from 400 employees to 5,000 in eight years. How did you achieve your phenomenal growth while focusing on being a purpose-driven company at the same time?

OZ Minerals' company strategy is centered around stakeholder value creation and is underpinned by a set of principles and accompanying behaviors called How We Work Together. I think this is a key part of what's allowed us to grow in the way we have.

How We Work Together essentially explains behaviors that we want to see from our people. The expectation is that it is used by all our people, company-wide, as it helps us balance our focus on *what* is being delivered, with *how* it is being delivered. Six principles, underpinned by twenty-four behaviors, cement our culture and purpose, and shine a guiding light on how we deliver our work.

Each How We Work Together principle is an overarching statement that speaks to innovating, including, collaborating, planning, delivering, and integrity. As we operate a devolved model at OZ Minerals, How We Work Together aligns our workforce and our culture.

We built How We Work Together in 2018 and it was based on extensive research. The principles and behaviors were focused on driving a diverse and inclusive culture from multiple angles. It helped us clearly explain *what* we were trying to achieve and identify the levers that we believe we need to concentrate on to effect change. This was important because the concepts of I&D can be complex – I remember having conversations with people about I&D and talking almost about two different topics. So we started by unpacking what we were talking about specifically – how are we defining I&D, what does it look and feel like, how do we measure it and define success? This approach allowed our teams to tangibly understand what we meant when we were having a conversation about I&D. It also informed our action plan, and what and how we were going to measure our progress.

How We Work Together helped us understand I&D in three core ways – creating an inclusive culture that has the ability and capacity to lead and leverage people's diversity; bringing in demographic diversity; and recognizing and embracing the role of cognitive diversity – and we made sure that, as a company, we had the behaviors in place, so we were pushing the right things to get the outcomes.

Because we did the work on the framework, we understood what was needed in our culture to drive an inclusive culture that can bring in and retain demographic diversity and support cognitive diversity. And while we're still learning along the way, I think this is what has allowed us to grow while being a purpose-driven company at the same time.

How supportive was your board when you started with OZ Minerals, and now, regarding your journey to focus on various stakeholders and not just shareholders' value?

The board has always been supportive of our journey, for which I'm very grateful. They have been with us each step of the way and were prepared to learn together. This was what enabled us to get ahead of the "trend," as I think most companies would have somewhere in their mission statement, values, or purpose, some element of delivering value or benefit to their stakeholders.

We were able to wholeheartedly embed value creation for all our stakeholders in what we do and how we do it, ensuring it's part of the whole company's DNA. That's why it sits at the center of our strategy.

A few years ago, we also developed a set of Stakeholder Value Creation Metrics that provides a tangible assessment of how and where we create value. It also flows through to our purpose, further embedding a focus on value creation into what we do.

Our Stakeholder Value Creation Metrics consider:

- What constitutes value from our stakeholders' perspectives
- The data we currently collect
- How The OZWay (a simple model that explains how all the parts of OZ Minerals fit together) applies
- Our strategy, aspirations, and priorities
- Our purpose

The Metrics provide transparency on how we are creating value for stakeholders and the progress we are making.

Over the past few years, we have also been embedding and systematizing stakeholder value creation into our governance processes, so it is always part of how and what we do, and is not dependent on human drivers. In developing the Stakeholder Value Creation Metrics, we provide transparency on our performance, and they also form the basis of our company goals, thereby driving performance and behavior in support of stakeholder value creation within the company.

I think it is only when we are creating value for all our stakeholders that we will have a successful company delivering against our sustainability strategy and achieving our purpose, "Going beyond what's possible to make lives better."

What is your advice to other CEOs who are struggling to achieve diversity in their company even though they want to or need to?

Again, I want to emphasize that we are ourselves at OZ Minerals, still very much on a journey in this space, too. So rather than advice, I think what I can share are a few of our learnings and reflections so far.

The first is that change doesn't happen by magic. What do I mean? At OZ Minerals, we think about culture through a framework of behaviors, systems, and symbols. When we were thinking about creating an inclusive workplace that has a lot of diversity, we took a cultural lens and asked ourselves:

- How are our systems supporting or not supporting demographic diversity?

- Are the symbols in our company demonstrating that we're inclusive, that people can show up and be their whole selves, or are we sending a different message?

- And lastly, what kinds of behaviors do we need to see from our people in order to get the desired outcomes – what do people need to do in order to create an inclusive culture?

Without these systems, symbols, and behaviors working with and supporting each other, we wouldn't be able to shift the dial on where we want to be with diversity.

Also, I think you can't get all the great outcomes from having a diverse workforce if you don't first create an inclusive environment where everyone feels like they can bring their whole self to work; that they are in a space where they are heard, respected, and can fully contribute.

We were conscious that diversity is about visible and non-visible traits. We believe it is important that our people and those we work with reflect the diverse communities that we live and work in. So for us, it's as much about aspects of physical diversity as it is about diversity of thought.

In addition, a diverse workforce means everyone can be in very different situations and circumstances. A question we asked ourselves was, "What are we doing to make sure the right systems are in place to ensure that we're not force-fitting traditional or 'one-size-fits-all' ways of working on our people?"

Where we arrived at was that we had to provide more flexibility for our workforce. This concept of a fixed organizational structure and model of roster sets will be a thing of the past. We need to provide a lot more flexibility for people who work with us, whether that's employees or contractors. It could also be more of a contingent workforce that has a much greater opportunity to choose how and when they work – and that will be everyone, including frontline operators, not just technical people or leadership positions. It is about giving the individual more choice about how they want to live and work.

We have an opportunity to leverage diversity, and it is more than just valuing and including different people and perspectives in the workplace. It is about understanding how individual differences can add value along the continuum of the employee lifecycle, and deliberately creating opportunities for those differences to manifest constructively.

Magdalena Kosior-Molloy, COO and CFO, Holman Webb Lawyers

Magdalena has over fifteen years of financial management experience and expertise, gained predominately through senior management roles within consultancy environments, professional services, and corporate businesses. She is widely recognized for her thought leadership and wise counsel.

As a highly accomplished financial professional, Magdalena is also recognized for her ability to transform finance teams from underperforming "scorekeepers" into trusted financial advisers for the businesses she works with. She strongly believes that the key to success in building, motivating, and managing high-performing teams is found in providing structured professional development and mentoring.

Magdalena's consistent achievements in improving and developing financial systems and processes include providing insightful and strategic financial management reporting and advice for the businesses she works with. Magdalena's work as a finance leader has consistently shown her ability to bolster the credibility of her finance team and their operations across the business for various stakeholders.

Following her passion for working with people from diverse backgrounds, cultures, ages, and genders to enable them to realize their full potential at a professional and personal level is particularly satisfying to Magdalena. Her strategic and leadership skills have contributed to her success to date. She is both a valued member of the C-suite and a highly inspiring mentor for younger professionals.

In 2017, Magdalena was awarded CFO of the Year – Runner-Up in *CEO Magazine*'s Executive of the Year awards – and in 2018 she placed as a finalist. In 2020, Magdalena was one of ten international finance professionals asked to join Sage's Finance Futurists group – an elite group of leaders who embrace constant evolution as a necessity in the ever-changing world of finance.

About Holman Webb Lawyers

Holman Webb is a dedicated full-service law firm that was established in Sydney, Australia, in 1960. Today, we have offices in Sydney, Melbourne, Brisbane, and Adelaide. The common thread across all our practice groups is partner-led teams of experienced specialists who are accessible, available, and responsive.

Our clients operate in a range of industry sectors throughout Australia and include major national and multi-national corporations, small and medium enterprises, not-for-profits, and Commonwealth and State Government departments, agencies and services. Our clients tell us that we are friendly and approachable, and many consider us an extension of their in-house teams. In fact, so strong are our client relationships that many of them date back two or even three decades.

Interview with Magdalena Kosior-Molloy

Tell us about your corporate career journey from the beginning till now.

I was born in Poland at the beginning of the emergence of the human rights movement, and popular discontent arising out of food shortages. I was educated in Poland and was the oldest of three girls. As a young kid, I was fortunate enough to travel with my dancing group, predominantly in Eastern European-block countries. It was through these opportunities that I developed a passion for travel and exploration.

I attended the University of Lodz. After the first year of my university studies, the travel bug really took hold of me and I moved to London. I was curious about the differences between Western countries, although ended up choosing London predominantly so I could learn English. I believed that developing my English would maximize the opportunities available to me in my life, and potentially even shape my career aspirations.

I met my husband Brendan in London, where I lived for three years before moving to Australia in 2002.

When I arrived in Australia, I was quite devastated to find that virtually none of my qualifications were officially recognized, apart from my Business and Economics Diploma. Unfortunately, the qualifications that were recognized in Australia were unlikely to get me the type of job that I wanted, so I commenced studying at TAFE.

I had always been independent – so I worked in hospitality while I studied. It was a challenging time. I obtained my first break in the corporate world through an amazing act of kindness from one of the customers of the coffee shop where I worked, Lynda Bradley, who was essentially a complete stranger at the time. One day at work she asked what my plans were in Australia. I told her that I was studying accounting at TAFE with a view to obtaining the relevant qualifications to get an office job. I told her that I had applied for a few jobs but had been rejected due to a lack of local experience. She told me to put a résumé together and that she would help me with my job hunt. Although she was a complete stranger, she told me that there was something about my work ethic and attitude that had made her want to help me.

Three months later, she called and offered me a job. I couldn't believe it. I was overjoyed!

I started my first accounting job in February 2004. It was quite a nerve-wracking experience as I didn't want to disappoint Lynda. She had given me this tremendous opportunity on blind faith and had no idea about my capabilities.

Lynda was my first mentor in Australia, and I will be forever indebted to her. Unfortunately, roughly a year after I started, Lynda fell ill and left the organization. As time went on, I was offered another job opportunity, which I took. Fortunately, with this new workplace came amazing people, including my boss, Lindsay Sturman. Lindsay quickly helped me to build confidence, and I became the manager of a small team. Under his mentorship, I started developing and progressing in my first Finance Manager role and completed my studies while working with him. I completed my IPA Program and became fully qualified, and now have a Masters of Commerce – Professional Accounting from the University of New England.

Over the next couple of years, the company I was at grew. We merged with another company, and I was put forward to become a Group Financial Controller. It was at this time that I met Sheryle Moon, who was and remains the most amazing mentor. Sheryle asked me questions that I was uncomfortable answering, but which were designed to launch me forward. She asked me what impact I wanted to make, what my three key strengths were, and what my pitch was going to be. This is completely different to the Polish approach, which places a focus on credentials and qualifications rather than "the pitch."

Under Sheryle's guidance, I quickly learned that in Australia you have to "put yourself out there." She showed me how to network and introduced me to a variety of people. She insisted, however, that I go on a personal journey to discover for myself where my talents lay and what I wanted to do – as opposed to having others tell me. She explained that people actually want to know what you stand for. Sheryle referred to it as developing your personal brand.

I learned that there was so much more to a career than the job description of the specific role I was in. I realized that I could make a genuine impact – not only in my industry, but in the lives of other people, by helping them on their own personal journeys.

Given my background, I tried to help people who had come from overseas get their first job. I understood the difficulties surrounding this task and knew just how lucky I had been when I was in their position. Fortunately, I was able to offer a range of people work experience in the organization I was a part of. I took in people from Russia, Poland, Ireland, Holland, and more recently from Uganda – all of different ages and genders. All were financial professionals who, like me, did not have local experience in Australia and were struggling to get their first break. I had a real desire to help these people; I saw this as my purpose.

In 2012, I had the opportunity to join Holman Webb Lawyers, a mid-tier legal professional firm in Sydney's CBD, as a Financial Controller. This was a big change. I worked with the firm's CEO Greg Malakou. Greg was a fantastic leader who helped me so much.

Looking back, I know that I have been very fortunate to work with the people that I have. They all pushed me and helped me with my career progression. They never told me that I couldn't do something, and they helped me gain the confidence to speak up about what mattered to me.

As a Financial Controller at Holman Webb, I was more exposed to networking. I soon realized that the financial industry was dominated by men, especially when it came to financial controller and CFO roles.

In this role, I started attending more and more industry events, where I would be amazed not only by the knowledge of these other controllers and CFOs, but by their confidence. It then occurred to me that I knew what they were talking about, and that I knew what they knew.

Although I shared the same roles as these people, I did not share their confidence. I knew that I had the knowledge, so I engaged a coach to help me build my own confidence – which was especially important as I wanted to talk to my boss about career progression.

Soon after, I opened up to my boss and explained that I felt that I was ready to take on my first executive role. This memory still makes me smile, as I remember the courage it took to start that conversation with Greg. In previous years, I had undertaken performance appraisals and had been told that my next natural step would be as CFO (although I was never told when).

In setting up the meeting for the year 2015, my usual process was to create an agenda and email it to myself. Without being convinced that I would go through with it, I put the CFO role on the agenda. However, I mistakenly emailed it to Greg rather than to myself. The minute I realized what I had done, I panicked. I contemplated recalling the email but knew that he would ask me why I had recalled it – so I went through with it.

We went through the agenda, and as we got to the last item, regarding the role of CFO, I said with a very shaky voice, "Look, I think I'm ready." He responded, "Well, I agree." I was so surprised at how immediately supportive he was, although when I thought about it, I came to the realization that I had been sitting on it for so long that he was simply waiting for me to be ready.

So, over the years I've learned that I must speak up for what I want – rather than sit and wait to see if someone is going to put me on their agenda. I learned that things just don't work that way.

Greg said that we had to get the promotion approved by Holman Webb's Board of Partners. I knew when he was going into the meeting. When he came out, I was on the phone. He simply came in and gave me two thumbs up. Again, I was blown away. I would later learn that all of the partners were completely supportive of the promotion.

It was a very exciting but also terrifying moment. I suffer from imposter syndrome, meaning that even if I want to do something, I'm often scared that I might not be able to deliver. When I changed my title on LinkedIn I had messages rolling in congratulating me, which is when the panic really kicked in. I thought to myself, "There's no turning back now!" I was comfortable as the Financial Controller: I understood what needed to be done as part of the role. Becoming the CFO was an unknown entity.

Fortunately, and I suppose unsurprisingly, stepping into the role of CFO has opened so many doors for me. This has been the case every time I've stepped into a new role: I have met different people who have impacted my career in different ways and helped me grow.

I joined the Executive Women Australia group to gain insight into what it means to be an executive. I was approached by the group's leader, Tara Cheesman, who asked me to talk to the group about "Why 2015 has been the best year of my career so far" (the year I became CFO). I told her that I wasn't able to do it. I didn't think that I'd be able to stand in front of eighty women and talk about my journey and my role as a CFO.

While it may not have felt like it at the time, I was fortunate that, like so many others before her, the event organizer was so strong and supportive about me doing the presentation (in fact, she had already prepared the invitation) that I felt that I had no choice. I recall being incredibly stressed on the day of the presentation. I almost phoned in sick, but I didn't.

For ten minutes I was supposed to talk about my career in front of this huge room of executive women, including the CEO of Ogily PR, who was also a presenter that day. It was my first public-speaking event, and those who attended gave me such amazing feedback that I was asked to present again three months later, to another eighty women!

Following on, I started connecting with these women that I had presented to. Many would speak about their challenges and what we can do to improve diversity at senior levels. We all agreed that, as women, reaching the top of our organizations had led to a certain level of loneliness.

At the time, I hadn't really considered that I might eventually join the C-suite, as there was no one like me sitting at the table. As a young, quiet, Polish mother, corporate boards were not representative of me.

Over the years I have undertaken several mentoring programs and have had countless formal and informal chats with males and females, although I have always felt more comfortable confiding in women with whom I share similar experiences. It is through conversations with these women that I realize I am not alone. I know that many people go through similar thought processes and think that they are "not good enough." I know that there are people who question whether they truly belong at the executive table. This knowledge reinvigorated in me the desire I had to help foreigners when I first got my corporate job in Australia – I wanted to help people and mentor those looking to enter Australia's financial industry.

While avoiding any sort of gender bias, I do have a focus on how I can improve the uneven ratios and issues faced by women in top financial positions.

It was around this time that I was asked to present a CFO series event. They were running conferences and asked me to sit on a panel in front of roughly 180 CFOs. This was quite daunting at first, although I felt within my comfort zone as I knew the answers to the questions. Of course, I was still concerned that someone was going to ask a question that I wasn't able to answer!

I was assisted immensely by my personal brand and public-speaking coach, Colette Werden, who helped me understand both the purpose of public speaking and why I wanted to do it. I realized that I wanted to engage in public speaking in order to help other females realize that they could, too. I also wanted to help encourage women to speak up and represent themselves – especially at times when they might feel quite vulnerable.

As soon as I started to embrace this purpose, things got easier, and the public-speaking opportunities came flowing in. I still feel a certain level of apprehension when it comes to sitting on panels, as at times I go back to thinking, "Who am I? I'm just Magda."

In 2017, I was nominated for *CEO Magazine*'s CFO of the Year Award. I remember working on my application.

The questions were daunting. I honestly didn't think that I was "good enough" to lodge a submission. My boss at the time helped me – we sat down, looked at the questions, and just started writing. Greg told me, "You've done all of those things. Just put it down on paper."

I was so surprised when I was notified that I was a finalist. I was the only female in a group of four. It was exciting and scary at the same time. I was concerned that I would be put on the spot and made to answer questions.

The awards ceremony was held in Melbourne in November 2017, with 650 people in attendance. Fortunately, my husband and then sixteen-month-old daughter came to support me. I remember the host starting to announce the runner-up in the CFO category... and then calling my name. I remember walking to the stage, but everything after that is a bit of a blur. There were some photos, interviews, and articles published in *CEO Magazine*. People started asking me for my views on various topics, which led to further opportunities. It was at this stage that I realized I needed to start discussing the issue of gender equality.

When Holman Webb's CEO (and my boss) Greg Malakou started talking about retirement in 2020, he put me forward for the newly created role of COO. At that stage, we had been working together for eight years.

He said that I was ready, and I trusted him. The Board of Partners accepted the new role.

This new position as COO was quite challenging. It was a new role within the firm, so part of my responsibility was developing it myself. This was scary at first, but as I grew into the role, I developed a much higher level of confidence than I'd ever enjoyed before.

Unfortunately, even now in 2022, when I look around the room at industry events, I notice that there is still not enough female representation at the CFO and COO level. I recently joined a group of general managers and COOs and am the only female out of nine. Moving forward, I want to help highlight this issue and help other women gain the confidence to achieve what they really want in their careers; to put themselves forward and not wait for someone else to bring the opportunity to them on a silver platter.

So, in retrospect, the last twenty years have been quite crazy. If, as a young twenty-one year old leaving Poland, someone had asked me what my life would look like now, I could not have imagined that it would turn out the way that it has.

I have been incredibly lucky in meeting the people that I have. With that said, those people obviously identified something in me which they thought was worth nurturing – given their willingness to help me grow into someone who can now mentor others in the same way they mentored me.

What are the personal challenges you have experienced or seen others experience when pursuing a senior leadership role?

The greatest challenge for me was backing myself and putting myself forward.

There have been times in my career where I genuinely liked the organization I was working at and did want to stay – but didn't have the confidence to "put my hand up" for opportunities. I left one organization because someone else was hired for a role I was interested in, although the reality was that I hadn't actually informed anyone of my interest in the position. This was a big learning experience for me, as when I resigned and it came to my exit interview, I told them I was leaving because I didn't get that role – to which they explained that they didn't know that I was even interested in the position.

So, I have learned that I must speak up if I want something.

Another personal challenge was when I became a mother and had to juggle motherhood with my job. I struggled a little with my identity. I love my daughter, but I wondered how being a mother would affect my career path. I had worked so hard and had such ambition.

As a result, I suffered from post-partum depression – and as a consequence of that I struggled with questions like, "Am I a mother, or a professional?" and "Will I be a good mother if I go back to work?" Unfortunately, at that time there were many people around me who were clearly not on board with mothers of young children continuing to work.

I was extremely fortunate that Holman Webb allowed me to come back for one day each week when my daughter was six months old. Overall, it was great for my mental health, but I did feel some guilt. As my daughter got older, I increased my days. Life then became a struggle between work, daycare, and other child-related commitments – and then on top of all of that, all of the networking required in my role as CFO.

Through interviewing and talking to other women in the same position, I have come to learn that it is people like me who are the best candidates, as we are truly driven by what we do and want to succeed. Frankly, people like that tick all the boxes. I do notice that male candidates have a lot more start-up confidence than women. They always believe they can learn on the job. Women tend to only apply for roles if they feel that they have the right experience then and there. Of course, that attitude is holding them back as the only way to get experience is to actually perform a role outside your comfort zone.

I believe this is why men progress faster and earn more. Then comes the dynamic of parenthood, which predominantly falls to women (although I do see this steadily changing). It becomes a vicious cycle. I believe that we need to educate all children, from a very young age, that we are all equal and can do everything we want. We can share the care of and be great role models for our children.

Crucially, women shouldn't be challenged on whether they return to work full time or part time, or if they want to stay at home.

Another challenge is one I think that many women experience: our innate character of always putting ourselves last. We look after our children and elderly parents before we look after ourselves. I believe this flows over into the corporate world, which is why I think seeking out mentors and working with business coaches is of the utmost benefit to women.

I wouldn't be where I am now without the various coaches and mentors in my life. When I meet people for the first time, I often comment that they are meeting me as "Magda 2023" – but that they haven't met me as Magda 2002, 2008, 2012, 2015, and so on. It's all a journey.

They say "you need a village to raise a child," but you also need the village around you to grow and progress with your career to achieve everything you want.

Holman Webb is active in achieving gender equality in senior leadership and partners. When did this focus start and how was this focus achieved?

Holman Webb is always committed to achieving gender equality. We made sure our progress was measured on a regular basis so that we could track how we were going compared to other organizations in our industry.

In 2020, we established an Employer of Choice committee. The committee's purpose was to achieve various goals, including improving diversity and inclusion. We asked staff undertaking various roles in the organization to participate and put themselves forward if they wanted to be committee members. We had equal male and female representation, and some short-term goals were to actively recruit and develop the existing female staff and remove unconscious biases.

During the recruitment and promotion process, the long-term goals were more ambitious. We wanted to achieve, by 2024, a 5% increase in the number of senior roles held by females. We also wanted to achieve greater gender equality at the partner level and improve diversity and inclusion.

What was great about this process was that all the goals, which came from the employees, were put into the strategic plan and presented to the management.

It was very structured and had a clear purpose regarding what we wanted to achieve, timelines, how we were going to measure, as well as a plan on how we were going to report on, our progress.

See an excerpt below:

Strategic Objective	Category	Short Term	Long Term
Improve diversity and inclusion at HW	Diversity and Inclusion (D&I)	• Active recruitment and development of existing female staff • Remove unconscious bias during the recruitment and promotion process	• By 2024 increase the number of senior roles held by females by 5% • Gender equality at partner level • Improve D&I

One of our success stories is that the last partners' promotions were all female.

Current statistics	
Females representation across firm	67%
Females at the executive level	75%
Female lawyers including partners	53%
Female partners	35%
Future female leaders (SC&SA)	59%

Was it a challenging journey to achieve such diversity?

Once we were committed as an organization and had solid support from the leadership team, it was easy to deliver on our goals. We had the framework and a plan; we knew what we would deliver by when and how it would be measured. We set several KPIs to measure progress and provided quality reports to the leadership team, which helped to hold us accountable.

One major success that came out of this process was the strengthening of our pipeline of female talent. In the past, we have struggled with women not having the courage to discuss career progression or to put themselves forward for promotions. Previously, women were not raising their own profiles within the organization – or externally within their respective industries. Very few were putting themselves forward for industry awards, which was another big challenge.

In order to improve our pipeline of talent, we put together a structured formal and informal development plan. With respect to awards, we are now more active in selecting, approaching, and supporting female candidates who have not had the confidence to raise their hands and put themselves forward when opportunities arise. We are also working on bolstering the individual profiles of our female lawyers in order to improve both the internal and external visibility of our female talent.

Holman Webb is fortunate to have a fantastic group of talented females, who, with the firm's support, have been working to raise their own profiles within their respective industries. This has in turn assisted our juniors, who are able to witness and follow in the well-calculated steps taken by those senior lawyers. Having real-world examples of successful career growth to look up to in this regard is exceedingly important for junior lawyers – especially for women who may not yet have developed the confidence required to get ahead in the legal industry.

Holman Webb also implemented a very structured mentoring program for the senior females in our organization. This sees our senior lawyers mentoring juniors by providing guidance on work, sharing stories, and helping with both career and personal development more generally.

Below is an excerpt from our strategic plan:

How does Holman Webb compare to other law firms and what would you like to see in the future for women working in Holman Webb Lawyers?

Holman Webb regularly participates in surveys to see how we rank against other legal firms in Australia. According to the most recent Australian Financial Review survey, women now make up almost one in three partners at the nation's largest law firms, which is a new record. Part of that survey rated Holman

Webb at number fourteen, with 35% of partners being female, nationally.

This is one of the areas within which we would like to increase the percentage of women, especially with such a fantastic pipeline of female talent, many of whom are preparing to take on future roles as partners.

When I think about the future and what I would like to see for women in the legal industry, I think big.

Flexibility is the most significant contributor for females when it comes to career success and progress, especially within the legal industry. When I say this, I am specifically referring to working arrangements – for example:

- Being able to work on a part-time basis
- Working irregular or changing hours from home
- Having support at home with regard to equal child-rearing responsibilities

Quite often, women in the legal industry excel right up until they reach senior levels, at which point they have children. This means that while women have their careers put on hold for a little while, their male colleagues continue to progress to partner level.

We have seen a shift in the workplace, wherein the new generation wants greater flexibility when it comes to working arrangements: people want the opportunity to both be a parent and have a career. To achieve this, we need to help male professionals build the courage to discuss with their bosses the need for flexible working arrangements, as well as the importance of taking parental leave in order to allow for their partners to go back to work.

That kind of conversation needs to happen now, to assist with the goal of gender equality. Leaders within organizations require education, so they can properly understand what their future leaders expect from them.

There is a trend at Holman Webb where men are taking parental leave so their partners can go back to work, and so they can be more "hands-on" as dads. It is important for staff to see real-world examples of colleagues (especially men) taking time off so the mothers of their children can return to work and progress with their careers.

What is your advice to other CEOs who are struggling to achieve diversity in their company even though they want to or need to?

Setting clear goals and KPIs is key to helping you achieve your diversity and inclusion targets.

My advice would be to make sure your organization is moving toward its diversity and inclusion goals; setting clear objectives with achievable KPIs are a great starting point. Encourage everyone in the company to be part of these important initiatives by having some notable champions within leadership roles. Communication throughout the process and regularly checking in on progress will keep you informed while allowing staff members to provide feedback that may offer additional insight into how effective (or not) certain changes or strategies have been so far. Remember – plans might need adjusting due to uncontrollable external factors, but as long as reliable information helps guide decisions every step of the way, then embracing change becomes much easier!

Felicia Gan Pei Ling, PBM, CEO, Ghim Li Group Pte Ltd (ASX:GLE)

Felicia Gan has been with Ghim Li Group Pte Ltd since 2006, starting as a legal officer and undertaking various positions including Chief Administrative Officer and Chief Marketing Officer. She builds, directs, and drives the annual strategic sales and marketing plan to achieve results in sales, market penetration, day-to-day operations, customer relationships, and order fulfillment. In addition, Felicia plans and implements marketing strategies to identify and develop new customers and business opportunities on a global scale. Since her promotion in 2019, her responsibilities will expand to include some of the strategic development and day-to-day duties of CEO office. Under Felicia's leadership, Ghim Li Group (GLG) will continue to build on its strategic direction, grow and develop the organization, strengthen its partnerships, and build new relationships. At the same time, Felicia will continue to retain her oversight over management of Finance, Textile Mill and Factories Operation, Business Development, Sales and Marketing including Outsourced Manufacturing and Product, Development and Design departments.

Felicia was conferred The Public Service Medal ("PBM") at the 56th National Day 2021 by the President of the Republic of Singapore. This award recognizes her efforts and GLG Group's commitment and contribution to the nation.

Felicia graduated with a Bachelor of Laws (Honors) from the University of Nottingham in 2003, was admitted to the Singapore Bar in May 2005, and has studied at Hass School of Business, UC Berkley. She is an Executive Council Member of the Singapore Fashion Council and a Director of the Textile and Fashion Industry Training Centre Pte Ltd.

About Ghim Li Group

GLG started in 1977 with humble beginnings as a sub-contractor with six sewing machines. Today, GLG is a global supplier of causal lifestyle knitwear apparel to major US and Canadian department stores, specialty stores, and mass merchants. GLG has over the past forty-five years reinvented itself to become an integrated one-stop service provider for the global textile and apparel industry.

With more than 9,000 workers across Indonesia, Cambodia, and Malaysia, GLG offers a total solutions package from product design and development, production planning and control, and materials management, to comprehensive post-manufacturing logistics solutions. GLG supplies an average of over 60 million garments a year through their marketing and manufacturing network. The company also maintains a marketing and sales presence in key international locations such as Singapore, Korea, and New York City to align with and seamlessly connect with their customers.

GLG is globally recognized for its service and product excellence, and has over the years received many awards from their customers. GLG is a Certified Women's Business Enterprise by WEConnect International and has held this certification from 2019. Some of CLG's products in the US carry the Women Owned logo to promote supplier diversity.

Interview with Felicia Gan

Your company has an amazing history because of your mother. Could you share that history of your company?

Since my mother started the company in 1977 as a subcontractor with six sewing machines in Singapore, she has built up Ghim Li's as a vertical manufacturer, from yarn sourcing, fabric R&D, and garment design, to knitting/dyeing and finishing, in-house printing and embroidery and garment processing of cut, sew and make. At the start of each season, we provide our customers with seasonal trends, design, and market intelligence services. With multi-country production flexibility and more than 200 production lines, Ghim Li is able to support short lead-time chase and replenishment with its vertical mill setup. We have self-accreditation certifications from our customers and are able to conduct self-inspections, and self-approve color and fit to reduce lead time.

My mother has built a good brand reputation for Ghim Li, and over the years, it has become renowned in the industry for delivering quality service and products. When I meet new customers, there is always someone who remembers my mother, Estina, dearly and will ask me about her and tell me stories of how hard she worked and how she supported their brands and found creative solutions to difficult issues. She always teaches me that we have to think of how to let our customers win first and that everything we do has to be centered around their interests, and enhancing value to them. She also frequently reminds me that, whatever promises we make to our customers, we must ensure that we are able to deliver on that promise and not fail them. With those teachings close to my heart, my team and I follow very closely in her footsteps and strive even harder to continue this legacy and excel in bringing our global brand to greater recognition.

How did you start being involved with the company professionally?

I graduated with a Bachelor of Laws (Honors) degree from the University of Nottingham in 2003. Initially, I did not intend to join the family business and I continued my graduation plan of working as a lawyer in a Singapore law firm. With my legal background, I was asked sometime in 2006 by my family to help the company as the legal officer and assist in the legal compliance, board, and secretarial matters relating to our public listing. Later on, I assumed the role of Chief Administrative Officer, taking on the Human Resources and Administration departments for the group. Soon after, I took on the role of Chief Marketing Officer, taking charge of business development of new customers and the day-to-day responsibilities for the Sales and Marketing teams. I joined the Board on 15 September 2015 and was appointed CEO on 1 July 2021.

When I started at Ghim Li, I realized that the textiles and garment industry is very dynamic with a fast-changing environment, just like how fashion trends go in and out of seasons. At the same time, it is very detailed and requires a close watch on things as we are always either in development or production at any one point in time. It requires strong teamwork and a meticulous eye to every detail, from fabrics, trims, and thread to washing and sewing techniques, at every step of the way. Even though I joined the company to assist in the setup of a new division for legal compliance, investor relations, and corporate governance, people development and talent management soon become my main task. What I enjoyed most was employee engagement and assessing the strengths and weakness of each individual as we continued to train and upgrade both their skills and mindsets to take on bigger roles in Ghim Li.

Succession planning and knowledge sharing within the company has always been my key focus. We have a large group of loyal employees who have worked for a long time for Ghim Li and have gained so much knowledge throughout their careers. Their wealth of knowledge needs to be imparted to the younger generation so we can continue to groom leaders of our future. We have earmarked individuals for training and empowered them with more responsibility, and at the same time, attached a few mentors who can guide them along the way. We are a labor-intensive industry and this primary focus on human resource management at the start of my career became an important stepping-stone in my future path to becoming a CEO.

How did you turn a family-owned business into a listed ASX company and why?

It was my mother's dream for Ghim Li to be a publicly listed company, as she strongly believes that in this way we can instill better corporate governance, greater transparency, and are able to attract talent to the company. She worked very hard in the 1980s growing our businesses and building factories across the globe, in Singapore, Malaysia, Thailand, Brunei, Fiji, Mexico, Guatemala, Cambodia, and Vietnam, to ensure that we have sufficient scale. Finally, she accomplished her goal of being listed in December 2005.

What are your views and beliefs for your company?

Culture is the essence of building a healthy and strong company. It is the personality of the organization, and it really starts from the top and inculcating the right values top down, through the organization, with our senior management, middle management, and leaders of our operations living and breathing the same mindset. We, as management, have to practice what we preach and lead by example to continue to inculcate the correct culture, behavior, and values in our organization.

My mother has built over the years strong company values of integrity, trust, and loyalty, and treats every colleague as though we are one big Ghim Li family. We recognize the value in treating each and every individual with respect no matter their position. As a result, we have a very strong, loyal employee base and continue to attract talent who values such a company culture.

You bring a junior staff member for certain trips out of the office including overseas trips. Can you elaborate why and how you implement it?

Exposure is very important to learning. As our main market is in the USA, they will need to learn retail and understand consumer behavior in the USA before we can market and sell our designs better. Visiting the USA is a must for sales and design teams. In addition, we are able to interact directly with our US customers and their design teams to better understand their design intent, handwriting, and brand DNA. Participation in such meetings also helps them observe and learn how to manage sales, design, and customers in meetings.

Please share your experience in embarking on your journey in sustainable practice for your company.

Sustainability has always been at the heart of Ghim Li and we have built special green teams within each of our facilities to promote and implement our core sustainable goals. The pandemic has resurfaced the importance of sustainability and we can see a rise of consumers who are demanding more sustainable products.

With the efforts of our green teams, we have seen our waste and energy come down by 20% to 35%. Since 2018, we have saved a total of 26,206.2 metric tons of carbon emissions by reducing our waste and energy usage, which we are able to give back to the environment and at the same time save some costs in the long run. We have already implemented a reverse osmosis water recycling system saving up to 30% of water usage. Going forward, we are considering plans to install solar panels in our fabric mill to do our part for the environment.

Over the years, we have been awarded sustainable accolades from our customers and are part of the Better Cotton Initiative (BCI) and partners of the Cotton Leads Initiatives (LEAD). Our Mill is also certified by internationally recognized bodies like the Global Organic Textiles Standard (GOTS), the Global Recycle Standard (GRS), and Step by Oekeo-Tex.

During the pandemic, we collaborated with Nanyang Technological University, Singapore (NTU), to develop a sustainable plant-based antimicrobial called ULTRA BACHTECH™ that is able to kill 99.99% of viruses and bacteria. This biotechnology is a clean-label, green product with no toxic or harsh chemicals, and it is eco-friendly. The natural antimicrobial compound developed by NTU scientists contains powerful antioxidants found in certain parts of plants. In lab tests done at NTU, the compound kills 99% of harmful bacteria by disrupting their cell walls. The research efforts from NTU have yielded a valuable resource for Singapore in the fight against infectious diseases. This innovation was an unexpected result of research in food science being applied in reusable masks used in the fight against Covid-19. The masks were distributed to Singaporeans and permanent residents in

March and May of 2020 as part of the government's strategy to combat the Covid-19 pandemic.

We have since further developed this and have successfully applied it not only on fabric facemasks but also gloves and medical uniforms and other PPE equipment. We are now further developing functional fabrics which have sustainable antimicrobial activity but at the same time have wicking abilities to absorb sweat, as well as being water/stain repellent with anion functions. Such functional tech fabrics are trending in the market, and we believe that in future consumers are looking for more "smart" fabrics that have multi-functions to complement their active lives.

The road to sustainability never ends, it is a continuous-improvement cycle, and Ghim Li will continue to push forward not only in sustainable product innovation but also continue to ensure that our factories operate in an environmentally responsible way.

What is your vision for the future of your company in light of your focus on environmental issues?

At Ghim Li, we are heavily invested in being a sustainable company. Our vision is to be above the global standard of sustainability. We were awarded Sustainability Gold Status in 2021 for our work on sustainability for certain customers. To highlight some of our accomplishments, we have achieved a 30% reduction in energy usage, which also reduced 2,175 metric tons of greenhouse gases between 2018 and 2022. Also, we have a 35% reduction in waste from our recycling and 6S Management system. Thanks to our water-saving project, we have a 50% saving in water used in production. We have done this by recycling condensation from the broiler and by utilizing rainwater. Lastly, we have shifted to using post-recycled content in 77% of our hangtags.

We have many sustainability programs and certifications and we are a part of BCI, a program that encourages sustainable farming practices. Global Recycling Standard (GRS) sets standards for certifications and recycled content for OCS (Organic Content Standard) and GOTS, both to ensure the organic state of textiles, including the harvesting of raw materials. We source 100% of apparel and soft home sales from suppliers using the HIGG Index. We have OKEO-Tex certifications which allow us to call out the safety of our products and increase customer confidence. We have implemented BHive, a tool that allows us to monitor chemical inventories. We are also part of the Roadmap to Zero program by ZDHC, a plan which eliminates harmful chemicals from our inventory.

What are your views on ESG, even though you have focused on sustainability practices before it became popular?

There is a lot of focus on the "S" and "G," which causes a lot of distractions from the ultimate goal of "E," which should be the main focus. Sustainability is a complicated subject and there are many ways of being sustainable. Companies need to stay focused on the main objective, which is protecting the environment and ensuring that they start something, no matter how small. When Ghim Li started our ESG journey in 2016, we faced a lot of challenges, internally and externally, but with the environment in mind as our priority, even that baby step is important and you will soon realize as you take more that you are rewarded with some low-hanging fruit, which then makes taking the initial step feel worthwhile. It is a continuous-improvement cycle, and as you made your first three-year plan and then your next three-year plan, you will inadvertently make a difference to the environment, and help protect it for future generations.

What is your advice to other CEOs who are struggling to achieve diversity in their company even though they want to or need to?

Diversity has always been a great challenge to many companies. However, over the years, I have observed more examples of women in leadership roles and getting the recognition they deserve, and this will continue to grow in the future.

Employing more than 60% females, and with a female majority on its management team, Ghim Li has been a certified Women Owned business by WeConnect International since 2019 and has a specific focus on empowering all its employees through education, awareness, literacy, and training. Over the course of our company's growth, we have continued to encourage female leadership within the organization and, through training, education, and exposure, have successfully nurtured female colleagues to rise through the ranks to become our future leadership team.

Keren Paterson, Founder, Managing Director and CEO, Trigg Minerals Limited (ASX:TMG)

K eren is an accomplished mining industry leader and Founder of the Australian-listed company, Trigg Minerals (ASX: TMG). Throughout her twenty-five-year career in the international resource sector, she has delivered results across the resources value chain – from underground mining to leading multiple greenfield discoveries, project development, operations management, mining finance, M&A, IPOs, strategy advice, mining services, and non-executive director roles.

Keren is a mining engineer from the WA School of Mines (WASM) and holds a Master of Business

Administration in Economics and an Advanced Diploma in Corporate Governance. She holds a First Class Mine Manager Certificate of Competency, is a Fellow of the Australasian Institute of Mining and Metallurgy (AusIMM), and is a Member of the Australian Institute of Company Directors (AICD).

In 2022, she was recognized as one of the Top 100 Global Inspirational Women in Mining. She was a finalist in the Outstanding Women in Resources Awards for 2020 and was the 2005 WA Telstra Young Businesswoman of the Year.

About Trigg Minerals Limited

Trigg Minerals is exploring for forward-facing minerals vital for global food security.

Since listing on the Australian Securities Exchange (ASX) in October 2019, Trigg has discovered a world-class mineral deposit, Lake Throssell, in the Eastern Goldfields of Western Australia. Early evaluation studies suggest the project has the potential to become a top-ten global producer of an essential mineral fertilizer, sulphate of potash (SOP), which will contribute to feeding hundreds of millions of people for at least a generation.

SOP contains two important macro nutrients for plant growth – potassium and sulphur. It is vital for plant growth and in particular for high-value, chloride-sensitive crops such as fruit, vegetables, avocados, coffee beans, grapes, tree nuts, and cocoa. It is also particularly important in hydroponic farming and in arid climates, and where chloride build-up in soils is undesirable.

The production of SOP from brine that is some eight times saltier than seawater is largely sustainable. The traditional method of production harvests the vast quantities of available sunshine to produce a natural SOP through solar evaporation. This method has a very low-carbon footprint.

Current global demand for SOP cannot be met from existing primary sources, such as Lake Throssell. To meet today's food production needs, some two-thirds of SOP is produced using synthetic, energy-intensive methods to bridge the gap, even before future population growth is taken into account.

Projects such as Trigg's Lake Throssell are needed to ensure our global food security and for the world to reduce the carbon footprint of the food supply chain.

Interview with Keren Paterson

Question – You have accomplished so much by your early thirties, please share your career journey that led to your achievements.

At thirty I was recognized as the Telstra Western Australian Young Businesswoman of the Year. At the time I was performing two roles – Statutory Mine Manager responsible for 150 people in an open-pit operation, and Feasibility Study Manager for an underground gold mine.

I started out in the mining town of Kalgoorlie, Western Australia, in 1993 – living, studying, and working on local mine sites. I chose to study mining engineering as I had traveled through the Australian Outback with my family as a teenager. I had fun exploring abandoned mine sites, but I thought we could do things better – with a more respectful and lighter environmental footprint. I also enjoyed a challenge – and I simply couldn't think of a more exciting and rewarding career than managing mining operations in the Australian Outback.

I got my first job in the industry after completing my first year at university, just weeks after my eighteenth birthday. It was quite the eye-opening experience...

The safety induction was going along well. I was taking it all in. I was so excited to be working underground for the very first time in what was quite a traditional mining operation, with manually operated pneumatic airleg drills that weighed about 50kg – pretty much what you see when you see an old-fashioned photograph of underground mining. The gentleman taking us through the induction arrived at the manual handling part; he paused, sat on the desk, leaned over, and spoke directly to me and another female student mining engineer and said: "Ladies, if you need your typewriters shifted, just get one of the lads to do it." Needless to say, we both looked at each other with a raised eyebrow – we both planned to operate an airleg that summer, not a typewriter.

These days there's quite a significant training and certification process to complete, but in 1993 I found myself shot-firing as apparently I was sufficiently qualified – I was eighteen, tick! – and I was studying to be an engineer – that'll do! The shift boss handed me some detonators, a couple of bags of ANFO (explosives), and a charge-up kettle. I was instructed to strip the backs (roof) of the drive (tunnel) as it was too low, and not to blow up the underground electrical substation, which was just meters away. Nothing like learning on the job! Fortunately (or I was extremely lucky), I completed the task without incident.

After graduating, I began the next phase of a mining engineer's education, which required specific experience over the next five years to qualify to sit for the statutory First Class Mine Manager's Certificate of Competency (FCMCC). This included a minimum of twelve months working underground as an operator across all facets of an underground operation – truck driving, bogging (underground loader), drilling, and blasting. I loved it – being down the end of a drive, on my own, hundreds of meters below the surface and deep inside the ore body was both awe inspiring and exhilarating.

The Telstra Award was a watershed moment in my career. I was nearing the completion of my Masters of Business Administration (MBA) and I came to the attention of a private equity firm that was just beginning to make its mark on the sector, Resource Capital Funds (RCF). This led to a stint working as an international mining analyst, where I would conduct due-diligence investigations and investment recommendations into exploration and mining projects on behalf of the fund. It was also the first time I got paid to fly in helicopters – you couldn't wipe the grin off my face on those days!

This was followed by a role in a copper mining company where I was responsible for the execution of its inorganic strategic growth. The first target was the company's major shareholder and owner of numerous assets throughout the world. This large and complex multi-jurisdictional transaction would have doubled the market capitalization of the business and transformed it into a diversified miner. Unfortunately, just as the transaction was being completed, the Global Financial Crisis took hold and, with insufficient working capital to adjust to the plunging copper price, the business entered administration.

This led to my first period of unplanned unemployment, where I very nearly lost my recently purchased house. This was a massive shock to someone who had only ever been told that I had it set as a mining engineer in WA – I was never supposed to be without a job!

So I learned to network and network I did. It was a tough time in the sector, but I worked hard and found myself with an opportunity to lead a spin-out of a company through an Initial IPO on the ASX as Managing Director and CEO. The year was 2009 and I was thirty-four years of age.

What was your experience with the gender pay gap?

My first experience was following our first summer vacation period at university. On returning to campus, I learned that many of my male colleagues had been paid twice what I received. We were doing the same work, with the same level of knowledge and experience.

I also experienced this in my first graduate role. There, I was paid a base salary from head office and it was up to the sites to "make up" the salary gap between the graduate rate and the operator rate for the work that I was doing. I knew that other male graduates that had worked at that mine before me had received the top-up payment. I stated my case and asked to be topped up to the lowest level trainee operator in the mine for the duration of my time working as an operator, no matter what work I was performing. I was told that I was "getting 'my time' toward my FCMCC and I should just be grateful."

On a third occasion, I was employed to project manage a feasibility study on a new underground mine. Not long into the role, I was asked to take on the management of the mining operations in addition to overseeing the feasibility study. This new role required my FCMCC and had statutory accountability. I benchmarked the role (it was paid 50% more than the feasibility role), prepared my case for a pay rise, and negotiated as hard as I have ever negotiated. I wasn't asking to be compensated for doing both roles – I was simply looking for the industry standard for the statutory role, where I was now leading a team of 150 people, managing a multi-million-dollar budget, and was personally accountable for their safety (I could have gone to jail if something terrible had gone wrong). The response – I was getting experience and I should just be grateful...

I would also like to mention that there were notable exceptions in my career where my gender had no bearing whatsoever on what I was paid. In these situations, they saw my skills, knowledge, experience, drive, and grit for what they are, and what I could do in achieving the company's objectives. They paid me accordingly and fairly. These are the men I am grateful to have worked for.

What were the challenges when you were looking for a new CEO role?

The success in my first role as Managing Director and CEO was abruptly halted by the Fukushima nuclear disaster. The company had recently made a substantial greenfields uranium discovery and was on the up and up, but quickly needed to pivot in a direction that didn't suit my skill set and drive, so I was on the job hunt again.

It wasn't an easy time in the industry. There were very few new IPOs and I was competing for roles within a wide pool of mostly male candidates. I explored all sorts of work opportunities – in Australia, overseas, in operations, and in government, and I started a consulting business to keep the wolves from the door.

But I was at a loss: why didn't my industry want me?

What led you to Trigg Mining?

While working as a CEO, I joined a group of other CEOs that met monthly to learn from and support each other. This group carried me through this period of uncertainty and it was their influence and encouragement that helped me to reconnect to my reasons for joining the mining industry in the first place – I wanted to do things better, I wanted to build mines communities could be proud of.

And as the Chinese proverb by Lao Tzu says, "A journey of a thousand miles begins with a single step." This was that first step.

The second step was possibly the most critical – I needed to find a company name and register it.

As I had been underemployed for some time, I had been researching my family history and found the story of my great, great, great grandfather, Henry Trigg, inspiring. At age thirty-eight and with a variety of skills including boat building, bridge design, lime-burning, explosives, and carpentry, Trigg departed England on *The Lotus* in the same month as the Swan River Settlement (now known as Perth) was established, with "anachronistic enthusiasm" for the opportunity that lay before him.

Trigg, a man of energy and compassion, was instrumental in establishing the settlement. He constructed many of the first public facilities, including bridges across the Canning and Swan Rivers to allow goods to be transported to the settlement from the coastal settlement of Fremantle. He was also known to be a tireless social worker, devoting much of his time to beneficial aspects of society and establishing and nurturing a church. His guiding belief was that energy and persistence are essential ingredients for success, and this is something I firmly believe in.[50]

That was 2014, and the company was listed on the ASX five years later.

How was the recruitment process that led you to hire a woman Chief Financial Officer?

At the time, I had three men and two women in board meetings and the other woman was planning to step down from her role as contract company secretary on the appointment of a full-time CFO/company secretary. In planning for the recruitment process, I was encouraged by one of the directors not to let the gender balance fall, and to search for a woman. I'm grateful he did, as I had been conditioned to think that my gender was something that I needed to balance out with a man in the CFO role. Yes – bias can occur in all of us!

So, my shortlist was 100% women in this case and, as a company, we are very happy with the outcome. For other roles, wherever possible, I've ensured that we have had a balanced shortlist and a gender-balanced selection team to address any unconscious bias we may have.

Was recruiting women and cultural diversity in a predominantly male industry challenging?

In the early days of Trigg, I found it difficult attracting anyone! We had no money, no exploration success – just some tenements and a vision. But once we'd identified the potential scale of the mineral resource and had completed an economic scoping study that showed the long-life, low-cost nature of our project, it became a little easier to recruit as our future became clearer and people were becoming more willing to take the risk.

I'm also competing with very large companies for talent, so we need to communicate the advantages of being a part of a smaller team where you have a much greater opportunity to see the impact of your contribution on the company's success.

When recruiting, I'm particularly focused on a person's fit. Our values and our culture are instrumental for our success. We need to make sure that each new person shares these with us as each individual has a much greater impact on the company culture when you have just five people versus 500, or even 5,000.

What is your vision for Trigg mining?

My vision for Trigg is to have a positive and lasting impact on our world. We aim to do this by producing low-carbon, natural mineral products needed for sustainable agriculture and human nutrition.

Lake Throssell is the very beginning of this exciting journey.

What is your advice to other CEOs who are struggling to achieve diversity in their company even though they want to or need to?

The first step is to look at the organization's values, culture, and purpose, and make sure that it connects to the values of a much broader audience – men and women. You might already have that – so, tick. The next bit is about looking at the broader talent pool, looking outside the current belief system of what the role may need, and looking for adaptability and growth mindsets which are vital in growing a business.

We've also made a concerted effort to establish gender-balanced shortlists. Mining is still male dominated, but this is changing and we actively look for women to ensure we are exploring the broader talent pool when recruiting for Trigg. This means we are looking at the cultural fit, skills, experience, and knowledge in a gender-balanced way.

Joe Walsh, Managing Director, Lepidico Limited (ASX:LTD)

Joe Walsh is a resources industry executive, mining engineer, and geophysicist with over twenty-five years' experience working for mining companies and investment banks in mining-related roles. Before joining Lepidico, Joe was the General Manager Corporate Development with PanAust and was instrumental in the evolution of PanAust, from an explorer in 2004 to a USD 2 billion+ ASX 100 multi-mine copper and gold company. Joe also has extensive equity capital market experience and has been involved with the technical and economic evaluation of many mining assets and companies around the world.

About Lepidico Limited

Lepidico is an innovative developer of sustainable lithium hydroxide and other critical minerals, and the global leader in lithium mica processing.

With a tech-focused, ESG-led business model that is pilot-proven, our first lithium production – from far less contested mineral sources – is due in 2025. The Phase 1 Project will provide a meaningful contribution to the decarbonization of the world's alkali metals supply chains. We are also working to grow our business with our second project, Phase 2. Other businesses have already begun to license our patent-protected L-Max® and LOH-Max® technologies, providing an avenue for royalty revenues.

Interview with Joe Walsh

How did you start working for Lepidico?

Almost by accident. Back in 2016, I was working as General Manager Corporate Development at Pan-Aust, where I had been for twelve years. We had built a very successful mining company from humble beginnings. PanAust's Chief Financial Officer introduced me to the CEO of a new private lithium venture called Lepidico, which was looking at undertaking a backdoor listing to provide access to equity capital.

I have spent a lot of my career involved with equity capital markets, particularly in Australia, so at first I was really just helping out a friend of a friend with advice on the Lepidico listing. While going through that process, I was asked if I could also help out by facilitating a strategic planning workshop with the leadership group at Lepidico, which I did. The backdoor listing had taken place by this time and the company had raised sufficient capital to really advance its first project study. Following the strategy workshop, I was offered the role as Managing Director. As much as anything, that strategic planning session was an opportunity for me to really get to know the people involved, work with the team to develop a five-year strategic plan for the business, and for them to get to know me.

Could you share some insights on your professional background in relation to your past experiences that resulted in seeing more women in typically male roles?

For most of my working career, I've been involved in an industry where there has been a reasonable representation of women in the workplace, aside for a few years managing seismic crews. Even if I go back to my more formative years as a child, I grew up in a stable and equitable family setting with an older sister and we were all very close. As such, there has always been gender diversity in my life, and I think probably more importantly, a respectful family environment.

I grew up knowing no different. However, once I got into the workforce, in some of the earlier years, when I worked in primary industries – particularly in oil and gas exploration – these were predominantly male-oriented business units.

It wasn't until I entered the banking community as a mining analyst that there was a reasonable representation of women in the workforce of the company I worked for, the Royal Bank of Canada group. There wasn't an equal number of female analysts to male analysts but there was certainly a greater representation of women than I had seen previously. However, it was evident that there was real equality among the analyst group. To me, it was a very professional and equitable environment.

It wasn't until I joined PanAust, where I was General Manager Corporate Development for twelve years, that I had the opportunity to really have a role in crafting corporate culture. During this time, we developed a really diverse organization and certainly diversity and inclusion became part of our culture.

We took that business from very humble beginnings as an exploration company with a large ground holding in Northern Laos. Our first project was a little heap-leach gold mine development, which we used as a stepping-stone, an enabler to develop a more ambitious copper and gold project. These mines were remote, in a real frontier region of Northern Laos.

We had very close relationships with the local communities, where gender equality was really embedded into their culture. The villages were operating at a subsistence level. Walking around and meeting the locals, you saw as many men carrying babies as women, for example. Women are very well respected in the community in these villages. They have well-established women's groups which have a voice in the community. When it came to employing our workforce, and if I remember rightly, we probably employed about 1,800 people at the Phu Kham copper-gold mine alone. In the whole organization we had probably close to 3,500 people, with most of these being Lao, employed from the local community. Furthermore, a good number of the workforce were women.

On one occasion, when we were fully operational at the large open-pit copper mine, we had a delegation of government and union representatives visiting from the capital, Vientiane. One of the union people asked, "How come you have so many women driving these 100-ton dump trucks when there could be men employed out of the community?" The government minister was clearly taken aback. He eyeballed the union representative and said, "If women can fly fighter jets in Israel, they can drive mine trucks in Laos." The reality is the women looked after the trucks very well and I believe they drove the trucks better than the men. The women were excellent operators. I cannot recall exactly what the statistics were across the organization as far as breakdown between men and women, but certainly we employed as many women as we possibly could on their own merit, as in many roles they were better performers than the men.

Reflecting on those years, I believe that these experiences had a significant influence on our corporate culture, and it was embraced both across the executive team and down through the organization. It came down to leadership. Our Managing Director was driven to have equality and diversity throughout the business. It wasn't only diversity from a gender perspective, it was broader than that. He pushed for diversity from an ethnic perspective as well. Therefore, when I look at our business here at Lepidico, where we are operating in Namibia and in Abu Dhabi, we have very different cultural environments to consider. In Namibia, we need to be mindful of employing people across a spectrum from different tribal units. In the mining industry, developing a mining business there, it is not straightforward to be only focused on gender equality as there are just not that many women trained and experienced for the more senior roles. That said, I think we've done a fantastic job so far, where we've got an all-Namibian in-country leadership team, which some other mining companies have stated is unattainable. It's not. There are some highly skilled individuals, for example our General Manager for Sustainability and Country Affairs is a Namibian woman who is in a Group-level executive role, and she has excellent international experience in senior roles.

It can be done, achieving equality and diversity, it just has to come from the top and really be embedded in the culture of the business.

Your operations include Africa and Asia. How did you recruit women in senior leadership roles?

I believe that it has to start right at the very beginning of the recruitment process and needs to be embedded via a diverse and inclusive culture. For Lepidico, we are building this business from humble beginnings as a start-up. Therefore, part of the brief to any recruitment agent is that we *need* diversity across the organization. For example, in Namibia where we are currently building an operating team, we want to establish both gender and ethnic diversity among the workforce, while also being in harmony with the community. I mentioned previously that there are tribal considerations in Namibia, where there's a significant number of different tribes, which we need to be mindful of.

There are not a lot of women in the primary industry workforce in Namibia, so it is a challenge for us for recruitment right now. We have developed a recruitment plan to build out our organizational structure over a two-year time frame, and in doing so will identify the roles where we're best able to achieve a diverse workforce. In time, training and succession planning will also be important features to become more diverse. As stated several times now, this drive really needs to come from the top.

For the roles that I'm responsible for recruiting, the executive management roles, I've been mindful of establishing diversity. If recruiting externally, the brief to the agent is to push for an equal number of female and male candidates, if possible. It does not mean we exclude men, but we do emphasize seeking out women candidates. For our interview process, we ensure that we also have an equal number of men and women in the final interview and, if possible, through the process. Having women in the roles of Chief Financial Officer and General Manager of Sustainability provides a good balance of skills on any interview panel.

Another example of our proactive recruitment approach is when we needed to recruit for a Country Manager. The interviews were conducted in Namibia and one of the candidates was a standout. It was very clear when I saw her CV that she was overqualified for the role, but she was on paper a very good candidate for Sustainability Executive, a role we were also looking to fill. Interestingly, I had a preconceived thought that the Sustainability Executive position would probably be based in Toronto, Canada, where we have one of our corporate offices. However, having this function in Namibia is a much better fit for the business since Namibia really represents the epicenter of our sustainability imperatives. It's where we have our greater sustainability exposures. Having a Namibian woman operating locally at group executive level is just fantastic. We interviewed the candidate, who subsequently came on board, and she is an absolute champion. She is brilliant for the role and brings great professional experience.

Having a woman as one of the most experienced and senior people in the country is going to give us the best shot at having as diverse an organization as possible. We are developing our business in the UAE, specifically Abu Dhabi, where it is not going to be easy either. We are seeing a real push for localization into the workforce for gender diversity, but it's kind of a similar situation to that in Namibia in some ways, although we're operating in the chemicals industry in the UAE. There aren't that many women in-country in skilled chemicals roles. Currently, our General Manager there is a man, but he certainly shares in Lepidico's values of establishing a diverse culture.

Right from Lepidico's earliest days as a publicly listed company when I first joined, the business was embryonic and there were only a couple of employees. One of my first tasks as Managing Director was to pull together a small but very capable executive leadership team. After my experience at PanAust, I was interested in having a diverse group and one of the first roles that we needed was a CFO, which is an ideal role in which to achieve some diversity. There are many talented female candidates in that area, even in the mining industry. As it happened, one of the projects I had worked on at PanAust resulted in me being introduced to Shontel Norgate, who was CFO at Nautilus Minerals and who was also based in Brisbane. Soon after joining Lepidico, I contacted Shontel and we met up. A while later, after she had come on board, she said to me that she was determined not to be interested in a role with another start-up company. However, after we met and had chatted for a couple of hours, she said to herself, "Darn, I've drunk the Kool Aid here." At that point, we were just developing our policies as a publicly listed company. Shontel is also the company secretary and is very good in the areas of governance. And that led to us developing a diversity policy very early on in the piece. Reflecting back, we've had diversity embedded within the organization right from the very beginning.

Following Lepidico's reverse takeover and listing, we went through a period of board changes to establish the appropriate breadth of skills to build the business and we were keen to have female representation on the board. Through Shontel's network, we were introduced to Cynthia Thomas, who is now a Non-executive Director and Chair of the Diversity Committee. At this point, Lepidico has a degree of gender diversity at all leadership levels of the organization, from governance at board level through the executive management team. Currently, the operating team is small outside of the geology and exploration areas. But those teams will now be built up and we'll do our level best to have diversity and equality throughout the rest of the organization and in all the jurisdictions in which we operate.

Your strategic focus in recruitment included local executive recruitment rather than just ex-pat recruitment in overseas markets. How did it become achievable?

I think pretty much wherever you work in the world now, there are local drivers pushing for localization of a workforce, and in most parts of the world that I've had experience in operating, that can be achieved. I was at a mining conference earlier this year and one of the other companies operating in Namibia said that they've achieved around 80% localization and they felt that they had probably hit a ceiling. I guess we're in a fortuitous position in the sense that we've got a blank canvas here. As discussed previously, we've started our recruitment top down and, as a result, have now recruited an all-Namibian in-country leadership team, and we've also achieved a degree of gender balance. I have two Executive General Managers in the country, one woman and one man. As a result, I think that we really have the best opportunity here to achieve as balanced an organization as we possibly can from a diversity perspective. I use that term more broadly than solely referring to gender, and I don't think that we'll need any expatriates in our business in Namibia. We will be employing about 140 people there including exploration. It is not a large workforce and it should be possible.

One of the issues that the mining industry now faces is there are really not many people studying mining, mineral processing, or geology these days, or looking at getting into these disciplines. It is seen as an old, dirty industry, making it difficult to recruit when there are not a lot of recent graduates, either men or women. This is something that needs to change, particularly given the future demands on mining for decarbonizing and meeting net-zero goals. Again, Lepidico is fortunate in the sense that the mining piece of our business is such a small part of the whole. We are much more a chemical business, which is totally immersed in the energy transition thematic, which is a fantastic drawcard for talent. Lithium is obviously vital for mobile electrification and therefore decarbonization, and that is really piquing people's interest as far as recruitment is concerned. Particularly in the last year or two, it's been evident that people see our business as being exposed to something that is new and exciting. Despite being a start-up company, we are managing to recruit quality talent for roles that are hard to recruit for, with candidates coming from traditional precious metals-based metals operations. Even though we are a small company in the mining space, I expect that we will continue to attract very high-caliber people because they are getting into a kind of new arm of the industry, and we have a compelling twenty-first-century culture.

How does remote working in your company work for you and your employees?

While being a relatively small organization, we have a global footprint. Our registered office is in Perth, Western Australia, which is where our technical capability is. Shontel, our CFO, and myself are based in a corporate satellite office in Toronto, and then we have a business unit in Namibia and another in the UAE. We span multiple time zones and we have to make it work. With the technology of today it is achievable. The executive team is generally flexible and at different times we all share the pain of doing calls early in the morning or late in the evening. For our team in Lepidico, everyone is very committed to the business, which is the key element that makes it work. And what drives that commitment is having a respectful, equitable culture. With a smaller group like we have at this point in time, that commitment is very tangible. The remote working piece does work and I think sometimes we maybe even attract better skills and talent by providing flexibility for remote working.

For example, one of our team members who was originally working in Brisbane relocated to Kuala Lumpur several years ago. Despite being remote from the group, Kristy has continued to work extremely effectively. Many of our staff travel extensively on business, which requires us to be able to operate remotely. However, some staff – like Kristy – have to travel regularly for personal reasons from KL to Europe and back to

Australia; technology and commitment allow this to work. With Covid, remote working was almost seamless at Lepidico. Funny thing is that we really don't know where some of our team members in the organization actually are at some points in time, but it does not stop them from being productive. I think we can, by being flexible in our working arrangements, actually attract better talent.

How did you overcome the recent Covid workplace challenges that make it difficult to travel in order to grow your business?

With regard to these last couple of years, we were set up pretty well right from the beginning because of the requirements we had for operating in different time zones. We are far from being a nine-to-five business, we all have to have the ability to be able to work from home, so everyone was already set up when Covid hit. Therefore, it wasn't really a big challenge from an essential communications perspective when we were all suddenly locked down and working from home. In actual fact, it was the environment around us that became more challenging. There were external groups that we had had very positive engagement with where we didn't have engagement for maybe a year after Covid lockdowns started. It was evident that other parts of the industry and other industries were grappling with transitioning to the Covid environment. We really have spent probably two odd years, maybe two and a half years, all working twice as hard to make half the progress, but we have made progress nonetheless. Central to this achievement is excellent communication using technology and personal values; trust across the organization is vital.

One of the things that perhaps I should have woven in previously is that the approach that we have taken to developing a vision and values for the business was very deliberately simplistic, until recently. I was cognizant that this is a start-up business, with a very tight, small executive leadership group. However, as we transition the business into operations and cash-flow generation, we are going to have a much bigger leadership team. And it's going to be essential that the leadership team shares similar values, has a shared vision for the organization, and that this can permeate down through the business. Over the course of the first half of 2022, we have doubled the size of the executive management team and for the first time we all came together as a group in August 2022. We are working up a new five-year strategic plan for the business. This is our second five-year strategic plan, which will really be taking us into developing a multi-asset operating business.

On the agenda for that executive strategic planning week, we had cultural development for the business, including development of vision and values for which everyone has to be involved. It is important that every

executive has ownership in our cultural development and strategic plan, which should then bring
inclusion into the business and make this part of the
business's DNA. Now we are at the point where we
have the leadership group in place that will take us
into operations and we can develop the right culture
for the business, which includes our collective vision
and values. It doesn't happen overnight and you cannot just do it in a two-hour brainstorming workshop.
It will evolve with time, but we have already made
some really good inroads. It's a journey; something
that will develop over the course of the next couple
of years.

**Why do you care so much about diversity, equity,
and inclusion?**

I think diversity is fundamental because our communities are diverse, therefore organizations should
reflect that. Furthermore, from a family perspective,
I have two teenage daughters. The lack of diversity
and equality is something that they bring home to
discuss on a daily basis. If I compare all the messaging that they are exposed to at school and their values
with when I was at school, it is clear that teaching the
curriculum has really evolved. They are growing up
in a world that is a lot more inclusive and sensitive
to diversity and equality issues. I want to see them
growing up in an environment where there is equality
and they can do anything that they choose or want to
do. Once they choose their career path, I would like

to see that they have equal opportunities available to them on that path.

At Lepidico, we are looking to recruit 120+ people in each business unit, for Namibia and UAE. If we are to achieve diversity and gender equality in time, we need to look at training people across most of these roles. With our vision of employing local staff, we are going to have a fabulous opportunity to be running training programs, taking unskilled people to semi-skilled roles, and taking semi-skilled into skilled roles over the lifespan of the business. And as we experienced at PanAust, we can work with local communities to really improve quality of life, sometimes off a very low base, even a subsistence level.

Currently, there is no industry available to some of our local communities in Namibia. But our business, when the mine and process plant are built, will provide excellent opportunities for both men and women out of those communities. I would like to see a very balanced workforce from a diversity perspective, be it gender or be it more broadly from a tribal perspective. Again, I think that these values just need to be embedded, which they are in our organization.

As I've said previously, I think it does come from the top. I would like to think that for my daughters there will not be any gender barriers in their chosen careers. They are both strong and determined: watch out world.

How supportive was your board in your initiatives?

We inherited much of the board from the backdoor listing and it was an all-male board. We knew we needed to undertake some board rejuvenation to ensure the right skills mix for the new business direction. There were some directors who, upon the back door listing, had already indicated that they would be retiring anyway. We were all keen to get some diversity onto the board. We are a small company, so we only need a small board, which makes this easier. We achieved that really quite early on in the piece, and again, diversity needs to come from the top and it is much easier to achieve in the early days of building a business. For an older, established business that was maybe founded in an era where diversity wasn't generally recognized, it must be a lot harder. We are fortunate that we can be diverse and inclusive from our humble beginnings. We will continue to strive to have a diverse board, a diverse executive management team, and diverse business units.

I do want to stress that it's not easy. I am mindful that we need to consider expanding the board to meet emerging business needs and we will be probably looking at making new appointments over the next year or two. We currently have four board members, one woman and three men. We will probably be looking at adding two new board members in time. This being the case, we should have an opportunity to achieve equality on the board.

It isn't easy to find the right caliber women who actually want to take on board roles. We have identified two women who would be absolutely ideal and complementary from a skills perspective at board level and who are real advocates for diversity. However, neither wanted board responsibilities in publicly listed companies, which is clearly a personal choice of theirs. It is challenging, particularly in mining, where there is not a big, diverse pool to be drawn from. Anyway, watch this space! We're on it and I'm sure that we'll get there.

What is your advice to other CEOs who are struggling to achieve diversity in their company even though they want to or need to?

At Lepidico, we took the view from inception as a publicly listed company that affirmative action does not work. In our society, this has generally been understood for a good few decades. Tokenism absolutely does not work. It is vital to have a well-conceived organizational structure and understand where flexibility in working arrangements can be afforded. Company culture invariably comes across in any interview situation, which makes appropriate cultural development essential for achieving organizational objectives. Candidates need to see that employers are walking the talk.

We discussed a little earlier about having people working remotely, and having people working flexi-time as well. You have to be able to trust your people, which then does open up a broader pool of talent. If we can maximize the use of technology for communications, then it broadens out the talent options. This in turn provides the best opportunity for having a more diverse organization. I really do think that it comes down to trust. And if an organization is facing challenges from a diversity perspective, then really some leadership refresh is probably required. Just one change and empowering individuals can have a snowballing effect.

My experiences over the past fifteen or more years really come from the perspective of business start-ups rather than from a well-established large organization, where the drivers are quite different. You should probably speak to someone else to get a view from that perspective.

Daniel Lai, CEO, archTIS Limited (ASX:AR9)

D aniel is the CEO and Managing Director of archTIS. archTIS stands for Architected Trusted Information Sharing, which is the challenge we exist to solve. archTIS is an acknowledged world leader in this space. archTIS addresses this challenge through the provision of data-centric security (DCS) platforms and products that deliver secure information access to content and collaboration systems. Daniel has been in the industry in both senior commercial and government roles for over twenty years. He is a founding member of the company and has successfully developed the business

to be recognized by the Australian and US Department of Defense as thought leaders in information-sharing strategies. archTIS recently won the Defense Industry Award for Cyber Business of the year 2022.

Daniel provides executives with strategic and architectural advice on how to gain a competitive advantage from their information assets across data, networks, business processes, service transformation, risk management, and security. archTIS is an ASX-listed company.

About archTIS Limited

archTIS Limited (ASX:AR9) is a global provider of innovative software solutions for the secure collaboration of sensitive and classified information. The company's award-winning, data-centric information security solutions protect the world's most sensitive content in government, defense, supply chain, enterprises, and regulated industries through attribute-based access and control (ABAC) policies. archTIS products include Kojensi, a multi-government certified platform for the secure access, sharing, and collaboration of sensitive and classified information; and NC Protect, a CP suite of products for enhanced information protection for file access and sharing, messaging, and emailing of sensitive and classified content across Microsoft 365 apps, Dropbox, Nutanix Files, and Windows file shares.

Interview with Daniel Lai

Question – With your multicultural background, could you share with us about your early life living in Canberra?

I was born and raised in Canberra, so I am a proud native. Canberra in the 1970s was just a big Australian country town. I'm half Chinese, my father came from Hong Kong to study in Australia, and had all the culture shock that comes with being an immigrant. There was even more culture shock when he met a Caucasian nurse and fell in love, I'm sure. They married and moved to Canberra to start his medical career here. It was interesting for me having that diverse ethnic background because when I was a young child, I thought we were very special. We were the only "Lai" in the phone book. My father later destroyed that perception when he said, "No, we are not special because Lai is like Smith and in Asia they are everywhere."

Certainly I felt different, and of course in the 1970s there were not that many Asians in Canberra. In fact, Australia's Asian growth experience at the time was Indo-Chinese refugees from Cambodia and Vietnam, and like all new-wave immigrants to Australia, they had a hard welcoming. It was a time not long after the white Australia policy. I grew up in a middle-class suburb with South African neighbors, who thought a good time was a knuckle dust-up over anything – it didn't matter what it was. It taught me you had to stand up for yourself.

I remember as a little kid, after being teased constantly about my name, that I wanted to change it. I decided to change it to Wing, which was my father's name: Chi Wing. I thought by doing that I would never get teased – after all, from what I could tell, no one teased him. So I went to school and told my class I had changed my name; that was a mistake because I got called "wing worm" for the rest of the day and teased outside of the classroom. Kids prey on difference; needless to say, I changed my name back quickly when I moved schools in third grade, I went from a Catholic school to a white Protestant private school; nothing changed, my brother and I were promptly nicknamed Ching and Chong. My brother was Ching and I was Chong. I was raised Catholic, went to a Protestant school, with an atheist father and Buddhist grandparents. I was confused.

So I certainly knew I was different and every time I entered the rugby field, or got onto a bus, I was often told I was different. I grew up in my early years with the feeling of not being in the inner circle. Fortunately, or unfortunately, I was quite a righteous kid, so I didn't mind getting into a little bit of a fight to stand up for myself, and particularly standing up for others.

These early life experiences instilled in me a couple of things – fight for the underdog, fight for justice, fight for equality, and don't be afraid to stand up for it. Interestingly, my father is a pacifist. He never wanted us to (physically) fight for anything and often told me that I should just walk away. I stopped getting into physical fights after primary school, but it didn't stop that drive and sense of fairness.

How did your early career roles shape you as a CEO you are today?

The goodwill of others has been the biggest impact on my career, and how I became a CEO. My grandfather lived and worked in Hong Kong and he used to write letters to me. He was entrepreneurial and I was fascinated by what he was doing from a business perspective, and the idea that you could be your own boss, being in control of your own destiny rather than leaving it to others. However, I was also extremely fortunate with the people that I worked for in my early career. They gave me opportunities and the authority to implement my ideas and run with them. That support encouraged me to take opportunities, try things, and not to fear failure. The cost of the fear of failure is the lost opportunity to succeed.

When I was twelve, I started going out and knocking on all the neighborhood doors, asking to clean their windows or do their gardening. Only one person said yes. I remember that the first feeling of earning some money off my own impetus was quite exhilarating, much better than doing chores like emptying the dishwasher and mowing the lawn for pocket money. The second thing that caught my attention was having the freedom to spend money that you earned on what you want, because it came with no conditions. That was real freedom. That inspired me to get my first real job with my uncle, Jim Murphy, in hospitality. I was working for AUD3.21 an hour serving drinks at a wedding with my brother and sister. A guest watched us work and offered my sister a job in her restaurant: "You're doing such a great job. Why don't you come and work for me?" My sister declined but I said, "How much do you pay?" She said AUD10 an hour: if you work like an adult, you get paid like an adult. I'm available, I said, and became a kitchenhand.

I did go back and work for my uncle many years later. He was running his own wine store, Jim Murphy's Market Cellars. Jim was tough and a hard worker, and taught me a lot about small business. I was a little naïve early on. I remember the first day that I arrived at his liquor store; there were wine bottles sitting by the door. He told me to bring them in and put him in the fridge. So I went in and I put them all straight into the fridge. Later, he asked where the red wine disappeared to. "In the fridge, where you said to put them." He said, "Didn't your father teach you anything?" I was so mortified. The next job he gave me was to take a box of wine across the road to the markets to do some wine tasting. I had never done anything like this before in my life. So, I set up the trestle table, I put out all the wines and I sat there. I returned to the store that afternoon and Jim asked me excitedly, "Tell me, what did you do?" I was worried I had done something wrong again but said, "Well, I did the wine tasting like you told me to." He said, "No, what did you do when you were over there, exactly?" I said, "I put all the wines out on the table and there was this guy at the fruit stall yelling out, 'Apples, *red apples*, 2 dollars a kilo and there's a great deal on oranges too. ORANGES 1 dollar a kilo.' So, I started yelling out, 'Free wine tasting, free wine tasting, come and get free wine, FREE WINE TASTING'." Jim was excited, "That's great! Because we've never been so busy; you're going back there tomorrow to do exactly the same thing again!" Of course, that encouragement led to other initiatives.

For example, I would review his accounts and noticed that there was a list of customers with a balance against them. When I quizzed him on it, he would tell me that they were all invoices that are owed to him. I said, "Why don't we collect them?" And I just picked up the phone and started calling the customers. He thought that was wonderful that I was collecting all his bad debts and chasing them up. After that, I got the opportunity to say to him, "Jim, people don't come to your store because you are cheaper than everybody else. They come because they trust you and they trust that you're the guy to tell them what wine to drink and which ones are good. You know what they like. So you are the business here. Why don't you do some advertizing and present yourself on television?" He quickly said, "No way, mate. I'm not doing that because that is not what we do here. We never know what return on investment we get from marketing. That's a 'no' because we don't have the budget for that." I said to him, "Well, what if it's not your money? Why don't we use Penfold's, Orlando's, or Lehman's budget, and you can do a deal with them where you're putting their wine on special and they'll pay for that?" Jim agreed. My friend, who was working there, and I set that up, and the adverts ended up going on for years and successfully helped grow the business. I guess what I'm saying here is that a boss with the ability to encourage you with an idea and say go for it is an extremely powerful thing, allowing you to be entrepreneurial and test out what works and what doesn't.

I took these lessons with me when I went into the music industry at Impact Records with Kate Robbie and Mick Telling. They ran Australia's largest independent record store in Canberra, and it grew from AUD1 million turnover to AUD5 million turnover in twelve months. We relocated the shop into the center of the city. I said to Mick, "We're getting all of this cash but people are asking to pay with credit and debit cards." He agreed for me to organize EFTPOS machines and left it to me to go and talk to the banks, get them in, and train the staff.

Around that time, the internet was impacting on music, such as the arrival of Napster. Mick was writing software programs for inventory control because we couldn't compete against the Top 40, so we had to look at our back catalog and inventory control was our competitive advantage. We then looked at how we put that online. How do we take our mailing list and convert? And can we sell music online? What other products can we sell? I really liked Mick and his leadership style. It didn't matter who came up to him and suggested ideas, he would always say, "Let's give it a go and see how it goes, and if it doesn't work well, we stop, but if it does work, let's have a crack at it." That nurturing style, to allow his staff to make some decisions and have a go in a safe environment, is gold!

I never had that feeling at university studying accounting. No one ever said to me, what's your idea about how tax should be collected? You either got your grades or you didn't. I was always much more excited about opportunities with direct results and that sort of encouragement, and I think that that really formulated my idea of what I wanted to do and how I wanted to lead a company. To be honest, I never intended to be the CEO of this company. In fact, I just wanted a place where I wanted to come to work, and I want my staff to have the opportunity to be better than they are, to be excited by their work because they are accountable for something; to feel that they can try something and have that same sort of support that I had. That's what really matters to me.

Your industry is male dominated, yet you achieved diversity in your board and senior leadership team. How did you achieve it?

This is Australia; diversity is our business. We just wanted diversity. It's how archTIS started. We all worked out of a tiny office in the early days. We were all around a table and we had this diverse heritage. We had someone from Chile, an Iranian, an Iraqi, an Englishman, a Scot, and a Eurasian guy all sitting around that table. Potluck lunches where everybody brings in food were great; we still do them. However, in those early days it was challenging to find female employees in IT, but it has gotten better. Our third employee was someone I had worked with in the music industry who worked in IT, Merryn Brown. Merryn inspired me to get into IT in the first place and was someone I admire very much. She has since gone on to build her own very successful business.

Still, the real driver of our success is our diversity in terms of males and females and culture. You need different perspectives. That's what makes a company great. Still, there's undoubtedly a different female-male mentality as well. You'd be very foolish to undervalue the different perspectives: that's like saying I'll listen to my father, but I won't listen to my mother. That's just dumb. I have been and am still influenced by many strong females in my life, starting with a very strong mother and grandmothers. My mother was an only child and always wanted lots of kids. The eldest child in my family is my sister, another force, so my brother and I were influenced by strong women. In my family, all the vocal parties were women. The men were strong, silent, and supportive.

I remember it was Women in IT week, and I was going to a conference. I was going to listen to a couple of different female speakers discuss their success and the challenges they faced in the industry. Before going, I reviewed our company's productivity. I started trying to work out the difference in productivity I got from my male and female employees. I estimated it was close to 20 to 25% greater for female employees. They didn't go on every coffee run; they didn't come back on a Monday morning and talk about sports for half an hour. They didn't take off early, they stayed back late. Of course, that is a generalization; we certainly have men that work very hard and long hours, but the point is there is a cultural difference. Take the time to ask hard questions – who are your best employees, what do they do, how much do they earn, and how committed to your business are they? It's not just good management; it's good business, so it's one of those things that you do.

I was also very fortunate that a friend of mine introduced me to a possible director for the company. I flew to Auckland to meet her, Leanne Graham. She's been on the board and very proactive about women in the business, but she's just a tremendous supporter. So, the first step was finding people I could work with, the second was ensuring they have different views and experience. This was the type of support I was looking for, not yes people; what do they add? Diversity and differences of perspective mean you will have conflicting ideas or priorities that must be managed. It means you must make time to focus, listen and evaluate ideas on merit. When you bring those elements together, you've got a strong foundation for a successful business.

Our Senior Software Developer is a woman. This week, we have a range of female graduates from the University of Canberra visiting the business for us to talk to them about opportunities and everything that we do, and how they can enter the industry. The dynamics are changing, but certainly, from the board level down, there is robust participation in ensuring that diversity is correct. The Chair is proactive in the need to keep the balance on the board and ensure that we demonstrate that through leadership when we look at executive positions.

I once had a conversation with one of our female executives who said, "It's not about behaving like a man to be successful; it's about believing in yourself to be successful." I have a daughter, the other founders have daughters. Miles, the Chair, has two daughters. Leanne, our Non-executive Director, was a single mother who raised her children on her own. We all want them to have equal opportunities and to be able to succeed in their own way. So, the thing that we look for at archTIS is your potential. Can we unlock it? Can you come on a journey with us for however long that is? And can we make you shine, and leave better whenever you decide to depart? And that's the basic philosophy of the business. One of the company's founders wanted us to be the Mercedes-Benz of what we do – he wanted quality. I wanted a place that empowered people to be better, and where the people would be the asset of the business. The third founder wanted to build a sustainable business. We thought we could do something amazing if we put those things together. So, why have an ordinary life? And that was where the philosophy of the business came from, and that's flowed down. We are looking for exceptional people, men or women, and to give them the opportunity to reach their potential and build a unique company. It's the chemistry between those factors that drives better creation, discipline, productivity, and critical thinking.

Was it difficult to recruit more women into your company?

The short answer is no. We never had a deliberate plan or strategy for attracting female workers into our environment. However, I think it was our interview style that attracted female employees; it's not a traditional interview style. We ask people what they are looking for in a workplace before we ask what they can do. We ask what they want from a workplace? What can they bring? What will make them excited? Are they going to fit in with us? One of our female programmers is now the longest-serving employee – female employees are very loyal. Anna has been given three pay rises without asking, because she wouldn't ask for them. That's not why she joined or stayed; it's the environment. If you take this approach at an interview and have a conversation with someone about what inspires them, what they enjoy doing, then you can talk about what you're trying to offer rather than the tasks expected in a job description. It's a conversation about people, and I think that has been more accessible and less threatening to people. We've always said you will never be bored and never end up doing what you think you will be doing. We will ask you to do other things and help you out, but we might sometimes put you a little bit out of your comfort zone.

I have always been fascinated by the confidence of men to try new roles or positions in the business compared to women. Generally, if you ask a man whether they can do something, their first response is "sure," even if they have no experience in it. From my experience, when you ask female employees that, they tend to say, "No, I can't do that, I don't have any experience in that." I find that it takes more encouragement for females to take on new challenges. I often point out that it's less about subject matter (you can learn it and we will train you) and more about transferable skills. It's about trusting your skills and capacity to learn. So, make them feel valued from the first interview, have a conversation not an interrogation.

What are your values and beliefs in creating positive impacts?

The most important thing about having values and beliefs is demonstrating them daily. I have a daughter. She is an incredibly proud female, and I am proud of her. She texted me one day and said, "Dad, there is a protest for women's rights against sexual harassment at Parliament House, and it is happening today if you can make it." So I went through the office that day and said, "Who wants to join me in going to the protest?" Our head office is only 500 meters from Parliament House. "If anybody wants to go to this protest, they're more than welcome." Some of my employees and I got up, marched out of the office, and went to join the protest. The head of HR is a real firecracker of a character and asked me, "Are we allowed to do this?" I said, "Of course we're allowed to do this. I'm doing it. Why wouldn't you want to do this?" She said, "But I don't feel right." I said, "Do you feel right about how females are treated in Parliament House?" She said, "No." I said, "Well, this is your democracy, and you have a right to protest." She thanked me afterwards. These things should not be something that's an exception. Live your values, don't just pay lip service.

I was in a discussion with the other founders one day about the CEO role – that I would only become the CEO if I had the support of the staff. So I went around the office and asked the staff, "If I become the CEO of this company, what do I need to do better? What

257

should I improve?" One female senior staff member who I always admired told me, "Daniel, if you want to be the CEO of this company, you can never raise your voice again because you are the company's culture. You must exemplify it and protect it." That, to me, was like, wow, and it just brought it all home.

How do you approach negative behaviors by employees?

I have a holistic approach. Confront it, discuss it from the different perspectives, and take action to change or remove the behavior. You can never necessarily avoid negative behaviors, sometimes these things do happen. For example, we had a brilliant engineer in the company, but he had an abrasive personality. He had a very short fuse. One day, we were in a meeting where he raised his voice and slammed his fist on the table. It was utterly unacceptable behavior, and it was directed at a female team member across the table. Before I could say anything, another senior leader jumped in immediately and said, in a very soft voice, that this was not acceptable and that he needed to calm down. This was a male manager, and he did that without any gap in time. I was very proud of him for doing that.

Next, we needed to address this issue, and we conducted an interview with him about his outburst. I had a discussion with the female employee after and asked her how she felt, and did she want to make a formal complaint about his behavior? Some companies will leave that up to HR and the manager to sort out. I felt I needed to be in that meeting to demonstrate that we care about behavior. I asked him, "Did you intentionally want to scare her? Did you want her to feel threatened? Did you want to dominate the conversation? What was it that you wanted out of that meeting?" He said, "No, no, no, it wasn't any of those things, I was just frustrated." I said, "Well, if that wasn't your intention to make her feel all of those things, how do you feel knowing that is how she did feel? Do you owe her an apology? Do you have a problem controlling your emotions? What support do you need to help change your behavior?" Negative behaviors do need to be confronted directly. It didn't matter what his intention was, it mattered what the outcome was.

We offered support to both parties. We offered him paid counseling because this was clearly an issue. Unfortunately, though, it didn't work out, but you have to stop that type of behavior. It sets in a rot. If you walk away from that situation, you're setting a standard from which you can never come back.

Tell us about "No Consequence Friday."

We have this fantastic HR Manager, and I promised her she'd never have a dull day in the office. We certainly have never had a boring day.

She was listening to a podcast called Radical Candor. It explained how we can be candid with each other. Be upfront, and enjoy the candor. Having honesty in our transactions and communications provides a stronger foundation for teamwork. You know you can go through the 360 or 180-degree performance review processes. It's all very formal and everyone is very polite.

Our HR Manager then told me about "No Consequence Fridays." It's a day where you can walk into the office and say, "I've had enough of this! You guys have been a pain in my backside all week. You can go to hell. Thank you and have a good weekend." I asked, "How are we going to manage 'no consequences Friday' if someone comes in and tells me I'm a dickhead or that they don't like me or whatever?" She said, "It's straightforward, Dan, we also have 'Repercussions Mondays.'" We embraced it. It was the ability to accept that we all have bad days, and we want to scream that out. It was the permission to have fun with all that tension and work you put in to try and achieve something together, and sometimes everything goes wrong. It humanizes your company to a level where you can shed a persona and be yourself, which is incredibly empowering.

It left everybody in the company going through the week with laughter, joy, and rejuvenation, leaving baggage behind in the office. I recommend it for only some companies, but it's up to the CEO to determine their culture and balance. But for us, as a start-up and the intensity with which we work, we're in each other's back pockets all the time. We still laugh about it every Friday. We run in, and we go; it is No Consequences Friday! And it brings joy to our hearts.

What is your advice to other CEOs who are struggling to achieve diversity in their company even though they want to or need to?

I've had some great mentors in my life. One of them was Dennis Richardson, who used to be the Australian ambassador to the US, was the Secretary for the Australian Department of Defence, and the Secretary of Foreign Affairs and Trade. I had a drink with him one day and said to him, "Dennis, what is the legacy that you want to leave for the Australian Department of Defence?" And he laughed and laughed and said, "What the hell are you talking about, legacy? This isn't about me. The defence department has been going on for over 100 years. I am a humble custodian, and all I can do is the best I can do on any given day." He asked me, "What do you want?" I said, "I want to be successful." He laughed again and said, "What are you talking about? You are already successful, but what does success mean to you?" And that's something that every CEO needs to ask themselves. What is it you want to achieve? Is it profit? Is it the status? Or is it a company that inspires it workers and customers? Is it a combination of all three? What are your priorities?

I started this conversation by saying, when the company's three founders sat down and we all asked each other what we wanted, I said I wanted a place that I love coming to work. I want a place where other people love coming to work. And self-reflection and asking yourself those questions are critical for any CEO to be successful. As Dennis said to me, politically, he could have been thrown under a bus at any moment by something outside of his control. There are many external factors outside of your control. What do you want to do for your organization that matters while you are in charge? So for those CEOs that wish for diversity, I challenge them to ask themselves what they are willing to do for it. A story I was once told really changed my perspective on how women plan; I don't mean plan their day or plan their families. I mean plan to go out after dark. To walk down the side path where all the lights are? What time can I get a train where I feel safe? Men don't ever think about that. Ever! We have a freedom that half of our society doesn't. So, what's the difference that you want to make and what are you prepared to invest to achieve it? Simply put, it is a priority or it isn't.

Vivek Bhatia, CEO and Managing Director, Link Group (ASX: LNK)

Vivek Bhatia joined Link Group in 2020 as CEO and Managing Director, with over two decades of experience in financial services, government, and management consulting. Prior to joining Link, Vivek held CEO roles at QBE Insurance Group's Australia Pacific division, icare and Wesfarmers General Insurance Ltd. He has also been a leader of the restructuring and transformation practice at McKinsey & Company across Asia Pacific.

Vivek serves as a Non-executive Director on the board of PEXA, which operates Australia's leading digital property settlement platform.

Vivek holds an undergraduate degree in engineering, a postgraduate in business administration and is a Chartered Financial Analyst (ICFAI).

About Link Group

Link Group is a global, digitally enabled business connecting millions of people with their assets – safely, securely, and responsibly.

From equities, pension, and superannuation to investments, property, and other financial assets, Link Group partners with a diversified portfolio of global clients to provide robust, efficient, and scalable services, purpose-built solutions, and modern technology platforms that deliver world-class outcomes and experiences.

Link Group helps manage regulatory complexity, improve data management, and connect people with their assets, through exceptional user experience that leverages the expertise of their people combined with technology, digital connectivity, and data insights.

Interview with Vivek Bhatia

Question – When you were appointed CEO over two years ago, you asked your board of directors for 50/50 equality in senior leadership. How did you achieve it?

It took time because I was prepared to take longer to find the right candidates in order to truly reflect the diversity within our executive team, rather than filling roles quickly. I've often found that it's in the rush to recruit that we compromise equality and diversity.

Were you worried about your board's reaction being a new CEO with your new vision?

No, I was never worried about the board's reaction. Partly because I have strong alignment in objectives with a very supportive board, but more importantly, I came into the role knowing that the board was proactively seeking change and transformation. Given my background, I think the board and I knew that it was a period of transformation for Link Group and that's what I was brought on to do. To that end, I have never been afraid to challenge the status quo, set a new agenda, and vision and mobilize the right team to get us there.

Did you experience any challenges in implementing your vision?

Change is always uncomfortable for people, and when you are working with such a large number of people in a global organization, there's bound to be a cohort that doesn't share your vision. However, staying the course and remaining true to your goals and agenda is important. Eventually they'll join you on the journey as they learn and understand more about you and your vision, or they choose to self-select out.

Either way, you need to be clear on what you're trying to achieve, what's required to achieve that (be it processes, tools, technology, products to people, and more) – and not waver from the vision, because true transformation takes time and perseverance. It doesn't happen overnight.

Your company has over 6,500 employees across sixteen countries, how did you successfully manage to achieve diversity in a relatively short amount of time being a large company?

Diversity has always been so important to me, so it quickly became part of my strategic agenda upon entering the business. I firmly believe that you have to walk the talk and do as you say, and not just have lip service. Therefore, one of the first things I did was to ensure that we included diversity targets as part of our executive and senior leader KPIs and that we opened up the diversity conversation at all levels. We have organizational diversity targets that are published externally so that we are accountable for our progress, and we rally harder than ever to celebrate and embrace diversity through events such as Diversity Month.

Was it difficult to recruit women in senior leadership teams?

We have a great business with strong fundamentals, and I think that has always helped us to attract talent.

Importantly, we actually have achieved a 50/50 gender diversity within our executive leadership team, which has further helped increase the talent pool that we attract. This is because anyone external looking in can clearly see that we not only value having diversity in our team, but we celebrate it. It's great for the women across our organization to have role models that they can aspire to, and that goes a long way toward talent attraction and retention.

What are your observations in regard to company financial performances since improving diversity in your senior leadership team and board of directors?

We have demonstrated solid and resilient financial performance since I joined Link Group, particularly given the uncertainties of factors such as Covid-19 and general market volatility. I truly believe that our performance has continued to be so sound in spite of all of this, because of the different views and perspectives that we've been able to leverage while navigating these uncertain times.

What are the beliefs that you have instilled on your children in regard to gender equality?

I hope that I've helped my children understand and see that anything is possible, and not just limited to gender but for all forms/aspects of equality, be it gender, ethnicity, sexual orientation, or disability. As they are now young adults, I want them to recognize that any and all the diversity that they bring to the table should be respected and that it is a real value-add for any organization they may come to work for.

What sort of future do you hope to see for your children?

I hope that they will appreciate the opportunities that growing up in a wonderful country like Australia has given them, and couple that appreciation with a strong work ethic. That's what my parents instilled in me when I was growing up – be a good person first and foremost, not to take things for granted, to work hard, and treat everyone around me with respect.

What is your advice to other CEOs who are struggling to achieve diversity in their company even though they want to or need to?

I think you have to make it an intrinsic part of your organization's DNA. Provide flexibility to allow a wider range of people the ability to work at your organization and attract a wider range of talent. Include diversity targets in your success metrics and consider if remuneration outcomes are appropriate to connect to these metrics. Last but not least – have open conversations about what the roadblocks are. When you can have a candid discussion about what needs to change, you'll be able to pave the way to achieve genuine diversity.

Be a Champion of Change

Now that you have read all the interviews, you have a sense of how committed these leaders are to advocating for women, not only in their organizations but also in leadership roles. If you are a business leader reading this, I hope that you feel inspired to be a champion of change in your own organization. These leaders have shown us that it is possible to create a more gender-balanced workforce.

I also shared the five strategies in Part One of this book, which was based on the interviews with these business leaders. They are a great starting point for achieving gender balance in your organization. But, as our interviewees emphasized, it's important to remember that there is no one-size-fits-all approach to this issue. What works for one company may not work for another. That's why the second half of this book features insights from these business leaders about their own experiences and how they achieved gender balance in boards and C-suite roles in their organizations.

I hope this book and their stories will inspire you to take action and create change in your workplace.

The time to be a champion of change is now.

References

1 "Gender equality rating on ASX listed companies," ellect.biz (nd). Available at: www.ellect.biz/ellect-star-rating-asx, accessed 10 February 2023

2 WEF "Global Gender Gap Report 2020." weforum.org (16 December 2019). Available at: www.weforum.org/reports/gender-gap-2020-report-100-years-pay-equality, accessed 10 February 2023

3 "Medtronic 2019 Annual Report," Medtronic, (nd). Available at: www.medtronic.com/au-en/about/citizenship/supporting-a-global-workforce/inclusion-diversity/annual-report.html, accessed 24 February 2023

4 Reiners, B, "54 Diversity in the workplace statistics to know," *Built In* (21 October 2022).

Available at: https://builtin.com/diversity-inclusion/diversity-in-the-workplace-statistics, accessed 24 February 2023

5 Parker, K, and Funk, C, "Gender discrimination comes in many forms for today's working women," *Pew Research Centre* (14 December 2017). Available at: www.pewresearch.org/fact-tank/2017/12/14/gender-discrimination-comes-in-many-forms-for-todays-working-women/, accessed 24 February 2023

6 Deloitte, *"Women @ work 2022: a global outlook,"* Deloitte (2022). Available at: www2.deloitte.com/content/dam/insights/articles/glob-175228_global-women-%40-work/DI_Global-Women-%40-Work.pdf, accessed 24 February 2023

7 Ibid.

8 United Nations Development Programme, *"Tackling social norms: A game changer for gender inequalities,"* UNDP (2020). Available at: https://hdr.undp.org/system/files/documents/hdperspectivesgsnipdf_1.pdf, accessed 24 February 2023

9 US Equal Employment Opportunity Commission, "Sex-based charges (charges filed with EEOC) FY 1997 – FY 2021," EEOC (nd). Available at: www.eeoc.gov/statistics/sex-based-charges-charges-filed-eeoc-fy-1997-fy-2021, accessed 24 February 2023

10 Reuben, E, Sapienza, P, and Zingales, L, "How stereotypes impair women's careers in science," *PNAS* (10 March 2014). Available at: www.pnas.

org/content/early/2014/03/05/1314788111, accessed 24 February 2023

11 Johnson, S, Hekman, D, and Chan, E, "If there's only one woman in your candidate pool, there's statistically no chance she'll be hired," *Harvard Business Review* (26 April 2016). Available at: https://hbr.org/2016/04/if-theres-only-one-woman-in-your-candidate-pool-theres-statistically-no-chance-shell-be-hired, accessed 24 February 2023

12 "11 stats from Sheryl Sandberg's gender diversity report that you need to see," LinkedIn blog (30 October 2017). Available at: www.linkedin.com/business/talent/blog/talent-acquisition/stats-from-sheryl-sandbergs-gender-diversity-report, accessed 24 February 2023

13 Waller, N, "How men & women see the workplace differently," *Wall Street Journal* (27 September 2016). Available at: http://graphics.wsj.com/how-men-and-women-see-the-workplace-differently/#:~:text=The%20disparity%20begins%20at%20entry,lion's%20share%20of%20outside%20hires, accessed 24 February 2023

14 Artz, B, Goodall, A, and Oswald, A, "Research: women ask for raises as often as men, but are less likely to get them," *Harvard Business Review* (25 June 2018). Available at: https://hbr.org/2018/06/research-women-ask-for-raises-as-often-as-men-but-are-less-likely-to-get-them, accessed 24 February 2023

15 Ibid.
16 Dixon-Fyle, S, Dolan, K, Hunt, V, and Prince, S, *"Diversity wins: how inclusion matters,"* McKinsey & Company (nd). Available at: www.mckinsey.com/featured-insights/diversity-and-inclusion/diversity-wins-how-inclusion-matters, accessed 24 February 2023
17 PR Newswire, "New BoardEx report shows only 5% of CEOs are female" Altrata. Available at: https://altrata.com/news/new-boardex-report-shows-only-5-of-ceos-are-female/, accessed 24 February 2023
18 Ibid.
19 Ibid.
20 McKinsey & Company, *"Women in the workplace 2021,"* McKinsey & Company (nd). Available at: https://wiw-report.s3.amazonaws.com/Women_in_the_Workplace_2021.pdf, accessed 24 February 2023
21 Buchholz, K, "How has the number of female CEOs in Fortune 500 companies changed over the last 20 years?" World Economic Forum (nd). Available at: www.weforum.org/agenda/2022/03/ceos-fortune-500-companies-female/, accessed 24 February 2023
22 Dunn, T, "Record 41 female CEOs among Fortune 500 includes 2 black women for the 1st time," ABC News (2 June 2021). Available at: https://abcnews.go.com/Business/record-41-female-ceos-fortune-500-includes-black/story?id=78046013, accessed 24 February 2023

23 Sandberg, D, "When women lead, firms win," S&P Global (16 October 2019). Available at: www.spglobal.com/en/research-insights/featured/special-editorial/when-women-lead-firms-win, accessed 24 February 2023

24 Lagerberg, F, "Women in business: the value of diversity," Grant Thornton. Available at: www.grantthornton.global/en/insights/articles/diverse-boards-in-india-uk-and-us-outperform-male-only-peers-by-us$655bn/, accessed 24 February 2023

25 "Women in the workplace 2022," McKinsey & Company (nd). Available at: www.mckinsey.com/featured-insights/diversity-and-inclusion/women-in-the-workplace, accessed February 2023

26 "A conversation with Maya Angelou," billmoyers.com (21 November 1973). Available at: https://billmoyers.com/content/conversation-maya-angelou, accessed 23 March 2023

27 Collins, J, *Built to Last: Successful habits of visionary companies* (HarperBusiness, 2002) and *Good To Great* (Random House Business Books, 2001); Collins, J, and Hansen, MT, *Great By Choice: Uncertainty, chaos and luck – why some thrive despite them all* (HarperCollins Publishers, 2011)

28 Johnson, S, *Who Moved My Cheese? An amazing way to deal with change in your work and in your life* (Vermilion, 1999)

29 Brown, B, *Braving The Wilderness: The quest for true belonging and the courage to stand alone* (Vermilion, 2017)

30 Dewar, C, Keller, S, and Malhotra, V, *CEO Excellence: The mindsets that distinguish the best leaders from the rest* (Scribner Book Company, 2022)

31 "Our Why", Z Energy (nd) https://znz-webbackendassets-s3bucket-prod.s3.ap-southeast-2.amazonaws.com/public/zenergy/about-z/documents/Z-Energy-Our-Why.pdf, accessed 24 February 2023

32 Ibid.

33 "Moving with the times," Z Energy (nd). Available at: http://nzx-prod-s7fsd7f98s.s3-website-ap-southeast-2.amazonaws.com/attachments/ZEL/392910/371745.pdf, accessed 24 February 2023

34 Simpson, M, LinkedIn post (nd). Available at www.linkedin.com/feed/update/urn:li:activity:6961820829219254272/, accessed February 2023

35 Nelsestuen, K, and Smith, J, "Empathy interviews," *The Learning Professional*, 41/5 (2020). Available at: https://learningforward.org/wp-content/uploads/2020/10/tool-empathy-interviews.pdf

36 "Diversity and inclusion," Z Energy (nd). Available at: www.z.co.nz/about-z/what-we-stand-for/diversity-and-inclusion/

37 Peck, MS, *The Road Less Traveled: A new psychology of love, traditional values, and spiritual growth* (Simon and Schuster, 1978)

38 Sharma, RS, *The Monk Who Sold His Ferrari: A fable about fulfilling your dreams and reaching your destiny* (HarperCollins Canada, 2011)

39 Brown, B, *The Gifts of Imperfection* (Hazelden Information & Educational Services, 2010)

40 Brown, B, *Daring Greatly: How the courage to be vulnerable transforms the way we live, love, parent, and lead* (Gotham Books, 2012)

41 Siegel, DJ, and Hartzell, M, *Parenting From the Inside Out: How a deeper self-understanding can help you raise children who thrive* (Jeremy P Tarcher, 2005)

42 Grille, R, *Parenting For a Peaceful World* (Longueville Media, 2005)

43 "#2 Be Water My Friend," BruceLee.com (nd). Available at: https://brucelee.com/podcast-blog/2016/7/20/2-be-water-my-friend

44 "What diversity and inclusion is really about," LinkedIn post (www.linkedin.com/posts/simon-sinek_perspective-activity-6752944125282152449-Pgo7/

45 Coyle, D, *The Culture Code: The secrets of highly successful groups* (Bantam Books, 2018)

46 J Siebel Newsom, "The Mask You Live In," YouTube (2022). Available at: www.youtube.com/watch?v=oN2W0fv8hY4, accessed 24 February 2023

47 Chu, JY and Gilligan, C, *When Boys Become Boys: Development, relationships, and masculinity* (New York University Press, 2014)

48 Salim I, Malone, MS, van Geest. Y, *Exponential Organizations: Why new organizations are ten times better, faster, and cheaper than yours (and what to do about it)* (Diversion Books, 2014)

49 "Read Martin Luther King Jr.'s 'I have a dream' speech in its entirety," NPR (updated 16 January 2023). Available at: www.npr. org/2010/01/18/122701268/i-have-a-dream-speech-in-its-entirety, accessed 23 March 2023

50 Devenish, B, *Man of Energy and Compassion: The life and times of Henry Trigg, Swan River pioneer and Church founder* (Wongaburra Enterprises, 1996)

Acknowledgments

Writing this book has been a journey filled with learning, reflection, and growth. I am grateful for the support and encouragement I have received along the way and would like to take a moment to acknowledge some of the people who have made this possible.

First and foremost, I would like to thank my husband and daughter for their unwavering love and support. My husband's encouragement and belief in me have been a source of strength throughout this process. Despite my daughter's severe physical disabilities, she projects pure love and joy every day with her beaming smile and determination to live a happy life. She inspires me every day.

I would also like to extend my gratitude to my editor, Jaqui Lane, whose keen eye and thoughtful insights have greatly improved the final product, and to thank Lucy McCarraher with her fantastic team at Rethink Press for publishing this book.

I am grateful to the CEOs and COOs who allowed me to intrude on their busy schedules and took the time to share their knowledge, experiences, and personal stories with me. Your contributions have added depth and nuance to this book, and I am honored to have been able to include them.

I am thankful for the Foreword that Ann Sherry AO has written for this book. She has championed the importance of gender equality for the past four decades while forging a successful career. Her commitment inspires me to push through the limitations and boundaries set by the business world.

Finally, I would like to acknowledge the countless activists and advocates who have dedicated their lives to promoting gender equality. Your tireless work has helped women to be recognized and included with men, and I hope that this book will contribute in some small way to the important cause of gender equality.

Thank you all.

The Author

Sandra has been advocating for women's rights ever since she was a teenager. She is the recipient of the Edna Ryan Award for Mentoring (for the advancement of women) in 2008, and was shortlisted for NSW Women Awards in 2018. In 2002, she became part of the executive team with BPW (an NGO called Business and Professional Women) starting out in vice-president roles in BPW Sydney, to State President for BPW NSW from 2006 to 2009, to Executive Director at BPW International between 2012 to 2014. During that time, Sandra was one of the Australian Leaders in the Commonwealth Business Council.

Sandra is also the only Australian selected to participate in NASDAQ's Spring 2021 Milestone Makers Program. As part of the program, she was showcased on the NASDAQ Tower in Times Square, New York City, along with twelve other outstanding entrepreneurs focused on the UN's Sustainable Development Goal #10, Reduced Inequalities.

On International Women's Day, 2019, Sandra launched Ellect to address the gender gap in business. In early 2022, Ellect launched Ellect Star, which awards companies for their achievements in gender equality in business. The purpose of Ellect Star is to highlight businesses that have achieved gender balance in their boards of directors and senior leadership teams.

Ellect is aligned with United Nations Sustainable Development Goal #5 – Gender Equality and Goal # 10 – Reduced Inequalities as a purpose-driven business.

To learn more about Sandra D'Souza, go to:

🌐 https://sandradsouza.me/

in sandradsouzaaust

f sandra.dsouza.ellect.biz

🐦 @sandra_dsouza

📷 @sandradsouzaaust